LEAN THINKING IN HUMAN RESOURCES

A GREAT PLACE TO BEGIN

By Michael S. Joy

LEAN THINKING IN HUMAN RESOURCES

A GREAT PLACE TO BEGIN

Copyright © 2020 Michael S. Joy

All rights reserved

Revision 20200421

I am reminded of my obligation to state that no part of this publication may be reproduced without prior permission from the author.

Lean Thinking in Human Resources: A Great Place to Begin

Contents

Foreword 6

Chapter 1 - Introduction 11

Chapter 2 – Critical Concepts and Tools 17

    Critical Concept – Business is Personal 17

    The Exhausted Traveler 18

    Critical Concept – Corporate Strategy 22

    Critical Concept – Problem Statement 24

    Tool - Team 25

    Tool – Charter Document 29

    Critical Concept - Time to Market 30

    Tool - Data 30

    Tool – Process Monitoring 31

    Critical Concept - First Pass Yield 32

    Tool - Systemic Thinking 33

    Critical Concept – Training and Strategies for Learning 36

    Tool – Process Flow Diagram 37

    Critical Concept - No System is Perfect 42

    Tool - Learning to See Waste 43

        The 7.2 Deadly Wastes 43

    Tool - Risk Mitigation 55

    Tool – 5S 56

    Tool - Waste Walk 57

Lean Thinking in Human Resources: A Great Place to Begin

    Tool – Bin List 58

    Critical Concept - Avoid Assumptions 59

    Critical Concept – Test and Measure 62

Chapter 3 – Applied Learning 63

    Our Mission 63

    Step 1 - Align with our Strategy 64

    Step 2 - Prioritize Focus 65

    Step 3 – Prioritize Project Focus 72

    Tool – Decision Matrix 72

    Step 4 – Defining our Project Charter 78

Chapter 4 – Measure and Quantify 86

Chapter 5 – Analyze - Improve Your Understanding 90

    Step 5 – Learning from our Factual Information 93

    The FourUp - Review of Our Process 94

        Quadrant I - Histogram 94

        Quadrant II - Trend 96

        Quadrant III – Project List 97

        Quadrant IV – Source Data and Implementation 97

        The FourUp Summarized 98

        Presenting the FourUp 100

Chapter 6 - Improve 103

    Three Ways to Improve your Indicators 103

    Step 6 – Problem-Solving 105

    Tool – Brainstorming 106

Chapter 7 - Control 110
    Step 7 – Chock the Wheels of Progress 110
    Critical Concept - Regular Reports 112
    Critical Concept - Seek Feedback 113
    Critical Concept - MBWA 115
    Tool - Post Mortem 116
Chapter 8 – Benefits 118
    The Benefits of Lean Learning 118
Chapter 9 – Challenge 121
Chapter 10 - Summary 122
Chapter 11 - Problem-Solving Tools – Translation 125
Epilogue 129
Acknowledgement 130
Appendix A - Checklist for Problem-Solving 131
Appendix B – Offered Templates 132

Foreword

This book was written for professionals that do not typically receive formal training on structured problem-solving or Lean methodologies and takes the perspective that these are foundational elements of leadership. Solving problems means making decisions and being a good decision maker is a leadership skill that can be developed and improved. A simple strategy for being recognized and growing your influence as a leader is to create a reputation of good decision making. To do that consistently, you can't leave it to chance. You have to understand the odds. You need a system that helps you make the best possible decision and places the best possible odds in your favor.

This book is intended to do just that, stack the odds in your favor. It is written in a coaching and lighthearted conversational style guiding the reader through a logical system for decision making. By the time you complete this book, you will be comfortable in the process and why the approach makes good sense. You'll be prepared to scale the approach to larger and therefore more impactful problems growing your influence based on a solid track record of real-world problem-solving.

This book will not attempt to make the reader technical and is presented in a natural flow for ease of understanding and implementation. We will convey the flow of good problem-solving to assist the reader along their professional path. We'll start small and local explaining systems for scalability to achieve results at all levels of influence. As we learn, have a little fun, gain comfort and make the concepts a habit, we'll scale our focus, impact and therefore, our influence.

This book is written from the "we" perspective which predominantly refers to me, myself, and I but also acknowledges all the people in my life that have enthusiastically shared what they know and made me a better problem solver. Everyone has something to teach and we continue to learn every day.

Along our journey, we will introduce a few terms to assist a shared language between the non-technical and technical world. We have a strong belief that shared language is foundational to strong collaboration across the organization, again, fostering expanded influence and harnessing the true power of diversity.

The approach in this book does not prescribe solutions. We honor the reader here and acknowledge that only the reader and his/her organization can determine what the right fit is for their company and particular phase in their corporate lifecycle or professional career.

Remember, people are always our most valuable assets and this book is meant to guide the Human Resource Professional through a process to recognize what needs prioritized attention. Professional engagement as demonstrated in this book will lead to improved business understanding, acumen and impact. Stacking up successes in this manner results in a solid track record of sound decision making and increased credibility.

You will improve your impact and your company's performance. In a global economy, a strong return on investment (ROI) is paramount to survival. Note that fifty percent of businesses fail in the first five years, sixty-six percent fail in the first ten. Further, there is no guarantee of survival after that. It behooves us all to do the best we can for our companies. The job we save might be our own.

It is virtually impossible to explain 'Lean' and have people truly get it, it must be experienced. You'll find the concepts are not complex and that often leads people to believe they're already doing it or they already know the solution or other common pitfalls. Most often, the gap that exists is the disciplined approach to true understanding. When a disciplined problem-solving process is not a habit, human nature has a tendency to move quickly to the preconceived solution. The most dangerous words in the English language are, "I know." Commit to start a habit. Empty your cup. Learn structured problem-solving and lean thinking. Recognize when you see that decisions are made out of assumptions rather than solid information. Hold yourself accountable and make your mantra, "good change starts with me" and point to yourself while saying it.

It takes meaningful repetition to develop a new skill and we urge you to simmer the celebration of the end of the project and instead celebrate how much has been learned about; the process being improved, the improvement process, the power of collaboration, organizational learning and ultimately, the decision-making process. Then take on another project. As these elements grow, so too will your success and the success of your business.

Note that the projects we're talking about could be a week or two long and done part time. The benefits of the approach will become obvious.

In this book, we will stress the entrepreneurial approach. Be the CEO of yourself and manage your career. Know your strategy and mind your business.

Who are you? How do you make money? Where are you going? What is your 5-year plan? Understand that you wouldn't be going there if you had already arrived. This recognition implies change, change takes time and requires resources. Resources cannot be squandered and given that the CEO is responsible for profit and loss (P&L) it is imperative that investing time into something should be born out of the highest probability of being correct. That this effort is the right place to invest resources. Leveraging the right information is critical to making sound decisions. The focused approach prioritizes time to work on the critical few items and keep away from the trivial many.

This book honors self-improvement providing an avenue to apply the tools to yourself and your business first or to your team if desired. We respect the individual and if you're choosing to apply this approach privately at first, we'll give you the tools to help coach yourself. To gauge your improvement and gain the confidence needed to continue along your path.

We would urge, however, that "the eye cannot see the eye" and self-coaching will only get you so far. To achieve next-level and true mastery, put yourself on a path to continue your learning, share what you've learned as well as teach others. You may be surprised who else has read this book, related books or has similar interest and experience. Collaboration almost always leads to better answers.

Chapter 1 - Introduction

There has been a shift in the corporate world that has been going on for many years. Made invisible by the pace of the transformation, the Human Resource (HR) organization is not staffed like it used to be. There was a time when the HR organization was a department with a similar size to departments like engineering consisting of 6-8 professional individual contributors that reported into a manager. The rule of thumb was to have 1 HR "partner" for every director. Consider that each director typically had 8-10 reports, who would, in turn, have 8-10 reports. The ratio ended up being about 1 HR resource to 50–70 employees.

These teams would handle everything from employee; recruiting, screening, interviewing, placement, training, professional coaching, reward and recognition systems, annual review process, facilitation of strategic planning sessions, relations, benefits, terminations, and payroll. The HR organization would also take a leadership role in various event planning and execution like company business update meetings, annual picnics or holiday events. They would also have involvement in making arrangements (or at least driving a standard approach) for hosting supplier visits or employee travel. If there was a death of a team member or immediate family member, they would often coordinate a signed card and perhaps flowers from the whole company.

They were well integrated into the company and had their finger on the pulse of employee morale. They would champion moral improving initiatives. These professionals put the human in Human Resources and were an advantage to companies that knew the impact they could have on the organization and how well it served its customers.

Times have changed, however, and the size of the HR organization has leaned out, to say the least. In many corporate settings these days, the typical ratio can be about 1 HR person to 400 employees. Some of the primary value previously provided by the professional HR organization, like providing one to one interfacing with the employees, professional coaching, mentoring and being an employee advocate, has been dramatically impacted.

Although sad, this shouldn't necessarily surprise us. Most organizations have a simple responsibility to be profitable. Controlling overhead must always be on the watch list in order to remain competitive in a global economy. Profitability ensures that your company is in business tomorrow to further satisfy its client's. Profitably satisfied clients create opportunities for companies to grow. Growing companies employ more people. Employed people buy houses, raise families, go the movies, eat out, seek further education and create opportunities for others which drives strong and thriving communities. Strong communities create strong states and strong states make great nations. Truly an ecosystem where good impacts create good opportunities.

We are not trying to make the argument that the 1 to 400 ratio is correct. The point here is that the HR organization has already been moved to a skeleton crew. Choosing to lean out the organization and build systems that allow the new HR professional to employee ratio is a forgone conclusion. The problem (or opportunity) is that the systems were not made to be self-sustaining or minimally supported prior to the change. That is unfortunate however it is reality. If you are an HR professional than from a self-preservation perspective it becomes necessary to be efficient and effective. The reason for this is because aside from assigning a bulk survey to have the finger on the pulse of the morale in the organization, the expectations for the HR professional role has not changed.

So, now that we know the HR organization is overworked, what can we do? Here's the good news, there is a lot that can be done to ease the burden of the new HR to employee ratio and at the same time, increase job satisfaction and professional credibility. Further, it doesn't have to be hard work. In fact, let's make the example project we work on in this book an effort to give ourselves more time. This book will convey the approach, the tools, and methodologies while simultaneously giving us back time so that we can invest it in our next initiative which will make a larger impact. Through practice, we'll gain peace of mind, personal job satisfaction, and increase our credibility in the organization as well.

Additionally, if your organization is embarking on a continuous improvement journey, don't be overlooked. Learn these concepts and demonstrate how HR can bolster the effort and role model the concepts.

Reality Check

There is a well-known fast-food chain that has been extremely profitable by being able to put just about anyone in a role and having them be successful in that role. It has become the conscious or sub-conscious model for companies to emulate. However, what companies envious of that fast-food chain need to realize is that the processes for those roles have years of continuous improvement behind them. The mantra for the salespeople selling this franchise to potential buyers is, "follow the system and you will be successful." What may not be obvious is that the systems are carefully optimized, standardized and documented over years of generational learning. This includes everything from how to make a hamburger to how to hire and train an employee. That fast-food restaurant approach has eliminated any need for real problem-solving or critical thinking for that fast food restaurant. Essentially, whatever the need, the franchise owner simply pushes the proverbial button and the outcome is as expected every time. That is a powerful concept and every company should be moving toward that end state.

The problem is that companies expect consistent output without making the investment into standardizing work and refining it based on generational learning. Adopting a problem-solving mindset that says, when something goes wrong we will implement a systemic solution such that the issue will never ever happen again. This isn't always easy but is necessary.

Warning: Avoiding the disciplined approach won't necessarily cause a company to fail instantaneously. More commonly, this approach leads to the slow decay of the company, however, the result is the same. Excuses can include; *"it's too expensive"* or *"you cannot have a system for everything"* and so many more. In our experience, these issues are not the reality. Rare are the companies that have exhausted all other improvements and the only opportunities remaining are large capital expenses. As far as not being able to have a system for everything, there already is and if that means nothing is in place formally, that too is a system. The real question is, "how much pain is the issue causing?"

In this book, we will discuss how to truly understand where you are, where you want to be and how to get there. We'll break the process of closing that gap into small, manageable chunks with a step by step flow for how to create your better tomorrow. The methodologies and tools shared are applicable at any level of the organization so as the reader, you may determine if you want to try the process and tools by yourself, in your team or across your organization. We'll do this in a way that starts small and local, then provides the knowledge for how to scale the process to larger scope and impact.

Chapter 2 – Critical Concepts and Tools

In the following pages, we introduce critical concepts and tools that will be utilized throughout the rest of the book.

Critical Concept – Business is Personal

Outside of Hollywood movies with Italian undertones, have you ever heard the words, *"This is business, don't take it personal?"* Have you ever used them? I submit that businesses are made up of persons and each person spends approximately one-half of their waking life at work making work very personal. Nothing could be farther from the truth and when we repeat bad output to a customer, eventually the customer will take that business personally and make a change to a new provider. For internal customers, that can translate into good people leaving because nothing is being done about continued poor performance and the costs of bringing on new employees shouldn't be ignored.

In the United States, and much of the world, we are a system based on capitalism. This approach is intended to reward the best providers with continued business and the opportunity to grow. Meanwhile, bad businesses should fail. There's no entitlement, no free ride, we get the business we deserve.

The Exhausted Traveler

Consider the following example. Think about arriving at your hotel after a long day of driving and facilitating the training on a new, and rushed, change to the employee benefits package. You've been working late for what seems like an eternity, you finally finish your last presentation and all you want to do is check-in, get a nice meal and relax. You arrive at your hotel. After not being able to find the reservation you made weeks ago, they finally get you checked in. You go to your room only to find it hasn't been made up yet. You haul your luggage back to the front desk and convey the infraction. After a few jokes about how *"this just isn't your day,"* they assign you to a different room. You're a little put-off by the dismissive comments and general lack of compassion but you push on, determined to relax. Certain that the issue will probably occur again to someone in the future but too exhausted to discuss, you grab your belongings and go the newly assigned room only to find the same unmade mess. You were right, it did happen again but you are surprised it happened to you, -and so soon. After all, they had weeks to prepare for your arrival and this is their profession.

Regardless of how the story plays out from here, what are the odds you will ever frequent that hotel again? For as long as there is a choice, you might not. Certainly, when all other considerations are equal, the choice becomes personally based. The key messages here are that there is a choice and that yes, business can be personal.

In contradiction, how does your perspective change when the first unmade room is responded to with sincere apologies, immediate short term corrective actions and at least the beginnings of what could be considered long term corrective actions?

Short term corrective actions could include; obviously getting you a new room, getting instantaneous support from a team member to go and verify the new room is in proper order, assisting you to the room by carrying your bags and opening your door, ensuring the room is to your liking, again expressing apologies and asking if there is anything else that can be done to ensure your comfort. Each of these actions has essentially no cost associated with them.

These actions alone might be enough to save the relationship. The hotel has the choice to take their solution further by providing an upgrade, offering your dinner complimentary or providing some other comfort intended to acknowledge and take ownership of the transgression. To create the sincere apologetic closure with empathetic ownership and conviction to ensure it never occurs again.

From a long term perspective, the hotel team member could share that there is a morning meeting and that this issue will be discussed with the intent for the team to consider the gap in their service, what went wrong and how together, as a team, they will implement change so that it never happens again. That we know you have a choice and we take any discrepancies very seriously. That the hotel's mission statement is, *"To be the provider of choice for business travelers to the area."* That we do that one guest at a time. We're sorry for the inconvenience, we will learn from this event as we continue on our journey to being the best provider.

What if the next time you stayed at the hotel, they left you a treat (better if they noticed a personal favorite) in your room acknowledging the past and that they remember you.

Even without upgrades or compensation, one approach dramatically increases the probability of future business while the other decreases the probability. There's a critical concept in here. It's not so much that things go wrong. It's how we respond when things go wrong. Done correctly, a solid response that puts the customer first can often create customers for life. Likewise, a poor response can alienate a customer for life. A good CEO recognizes those opportunities in their business.

To continue along this thinking, repeat business is the most profitable. Have you ever considered the cost of gaining new customers (this concept is quantifiable and makes a great metric), especially when you've achieved a bad reputation? Business is personal. Don't get yourself, or your business, in a position where you have to dig yourself out of a bad reputation.

Now, consider that if a certain department in your organization, perhaps your own, is based in inefficiencies causing other employees to endlessly search, redo or rework whatever it is they are trying to do outside of their expertise, then aren't we diverting good energy from where we hired them to make an impact. Can't that be as exhausting as lugging your luggage back to the lobby? Doesn't the supervisor of their primary responsibilities miss them?

Whether the employee is an operator on the floor, a maintenance worker, a custodian or the CEO, they were hired to do a job. Distracting them from their primary responsibilities and worse, wasting their time (i.e. broken links, dead ends, overly complex systems) costs money. The problem (or opportunity) is that often this type of waste cannot be measured. This concept is referred to as the hidden factory in manufacturing environments. Processes that create waste, measured or not, still cost money and that is a negative impact on our P&L. Left ignored, this too can accumulate and proliferate the message that squandered time is acceptable. Proliferate that message broadly enough and it embeds into your corporate culture. A culture riddled with accepting waste can silently kill your company.

Critical Concept – Corporate Strategy

The desire for immediate results in America is getting in the way of planning for long-term success. Many companies today want all the benefits of repeatable, reproducible processes that can be executed by anyone without providing the effort that goes into creating them. Further, an implemented sub-par process often results in mistakes. Mistakes are wasteful and simply must be reduced if not eliminated. Constantly correcting mistakes resulting from poor processes is expensive and indicators may not always be equipped to expose those costs. Left uncorrected, these hidden costs erode the business one dollar at a time. When isolated, it won't be long until someone figures it out and makes a correction in the form of a headcount change. When pervasive, it's a company killer and can be a self-perpetuating death spiral.

Investing the right resources into developing an organizationally synchronized and prioritized plan is foundational to long term profitability and growth. Strategy, for you or your company, identifies who you want to be and how you want to make money. The importance of a strategy that connects every level of the organization to who you are as a business and how you make money cannot be overstated.

Coach's Note on Strategy: *– Developing a strategy for yourself, your group, your department or your organization is crucial. It sets direction and aligns all efforts to move in that direction. Too many organizations are absent of a corporate strategy and the necessary cascading plans needed to achieve goals. As stated by the savvy Cheshire Cat in Lewis Carroll's, Alice in Wonderland, "if you don't know where you are going, any road will get you there."*

Once the company-wide strategy is achieved, the next step is to create department (or local) initiatives that align with the strategy. Those initiatives need specific objectives, ownership, clear deliverables including associated timelines. In turn, those initiatives need to flow to the next level of the organization ultimately translating into individual tasks at all levels. The goal is that every employee in the company completely understands what they do and how it aligns with the direction of the organization. These cascading goals provide connection, belonging and sense of solidarity across the organization. Nothing is more powerful than a unified approach to a shared destiny. Exploit the power of the team.

In this book, we will introduce various tools and a phased approach to problem-solving. The sort of problems we'll be solving here will be of a style where we've surveyed our environment, found some inefficiencies and we want to make improvements because of the excess work these inefficiencies are causing. These types of problems contrast with those that suddenly arise and need immediate response though many of the same tools would be leveraged.

Critical Concept – Problem Statement

In structured problem-solving, we like to create a deep understanding of the initiative and the problem that is intended to be resolved. A fundamental concept we need to keep in mind is that all the work we do must align with our corporate strategy. Energy working on something outside our established strategy is waste. In an effort to sing from the same corporate sheet of music, we want to document the problem we intend to solve and demonstrate its alignment to the overarching strategy. Next, we'll convert that problem statement into our stated objective. This action is paramount to aligning any team toward a common goal.

A common saying in the problem-solving world is that a well-defined problem statement is a problem half solved. It becomes the aligning force and translates into the objective that binds the team together. Keeping our objective in mind throughout any effort is key to avoiding scope creep and missed deliverables. When we consider our problem statement we should get as specific as we can without implying a solution. The problem statement should tell us; what process we're talking about, what is going wrong, how much has gone wrong and when it was first noticed. We should quantify wherever possible.

Note that we didn't state anything about why we think it is happening, or, when or how we'll solve it. At this step in the problem-solving process, those would all be assumptions and as a rule, we do not make assumptions. Assumptions come with the risk of the unknown, can be misleading and entice us, through the allure of a quick resolution, away from stacking the odds in our favor.

Tool - Team

Now don't get us wrong, we don't mean to refer to the team as a bunch of tools. Here they are referred to as a tool because of what they bring to the table to resolve the problem. Their competencies become the necessary tools to resolve the issue and ensure it can never repeat.

As we draw closer to the action we'll take regarding our specific initiative, we must derive the right team to engage it. Who should be a part of the core team and who might you need to consult with as a part of the extended team? What competencies and perspectives will be required? Will anticipated solutions require IT support in the form of programming or webpage modifications? Will this change require training, a communication campaign? Would it be best to include a training expert early in the effort? Do we have representation from the right audience that can accurately portray the process, participate in creating a better one and provide expertise for accurate resolution? You'll want a healthy cross-section of expertise and be reminded to balance the impact on people's time with the effort.

In an effort to provide calibration regarding team size, it depends and can be anywhere from 3 to 12 as appropriate. More than that for any project expected to take less than six months and you're in for a bumpy ride. Keep in mind that at this stage of our problem-solving learning curve, we're talking about fast and relatively small scale initiatives with a target completion of less than twelve weeks.

If you decide to pull a team together, you'd want to build the charter document as a team and one of the questions you'd want to ask in that first discussion is, "do we have the right representation in this team?" Adjustments can be made if necessary but the goal would be to lock in the team and keep that team through project closure. Turnover will impact the team dynamics often causing a reset and it will take time to gain alignment and momentum again.

In addition to competency, one of the most important things to consider in choosing a team is stacking the deck with positive, enthusiastic people who have a stake in the output. They will help shape the solution in the right direction as they know they will have to live with the output. Improve your probability of success by getting the right team together.

For as long as we have been in the professional world we've been an agent of change. We have observed change and its effects on people. Some immediately see the benefits, some seek it but most don't want it. Please allow me to repeat, "Most people do not want change." Some of those people may even be the biggest complainers against the current system but then they argue every path to the next and better version of the process. These people seem to love the comfort of their confines. They don't want to harness their own power to unlock those shackles and aspire to a better situation.

There's the stigma of not being able to teach an old dog a new trick, however, we would argue that most people do not like change, period. When push comes to shove and change occurs, the population breakdown reflects something similar to the standard merit curve. About 5-10% of the population will positively pursue change. About 5-10% will work to interfere with change and the remainder will spread across the continuum of willing adopters to those that just want to be told what to do.

The key point here is that you will encounter people that are resistant to change. Wrap your mind around the strongest elixir for fear of change, -collaboration. It increases your odds of long term sustainable change one hundredfold.

Play the odds and stack your team with those that are positive people, open to change and informal influencers to the group. It might be the worst thing you can do to simply build a team filled with people that have seniority, are your friends, asked to be included, had nothing else to do, or some other reason disconnected from getting the type of people needed to creatively think of, represent and pursue this specific good change. Eventually, you will pursue enough changes that anyone who wants to get involved can, but, in the early phases of introducing a change process, stack the deck in your favor and create those early wins. Refine your approach, garner trust, and build momentum.

Bring the majority of people up together. There will always be naysayers and they will eventually catch on. A great way to pause their negativity and engage them is to simply ask them to give the new system a try. That you've harnessed the wisdom of the crowd (a scientific study that says the collective wisdom of the crowd is more often correct than any individual). That the team worked hard to build a better way and to just try it in the spirit of discovery. That if we're not always improving, we're standing still which looks a lot like going backward when compared to the competition.

Tool – Charter Document

Charter documents become more important to an initiative the more complex the initiative is. It serves as a formal document to capture such concepts as; what is being worked on, why it makes sense to work on it (business case), who will work on it, how long it is expected to take, logistics, deliverables and more. We'll get into more detail later on.

Coach's Note on Charter Documents: Formal charter documents are available. They have many elements to them and can get very specific including team members, their roles, start date, expected end date, sponsors, key stakeholders, decision-making criteria, time expected per week for each role and much more. Charter documents are a powerful tool and they can get very detailed but they do not have to be. The solution should scale to the effort. For example, a charter document for a two-week project should look very different than that of a two-year program. A key component that cannot be skipped is making deliverables clear. When the deliverables are specific and quantifiable, there is no ambiguity for when the effort is completed successfully. It is the antidote to scope creep and when properly shared ensures alignment with the team, customers, supervisors, and other key stakeholders. Write to us at thejoysofbusiness@gmail.com for a free charter document template.

Critical Concept - Time to Market

Time to Market is a concept typically defined as the amount of time it takes to take a product from concept to making it available for sale. Here we use the word product in a broader sense applying it to what others are getting from you/your team. Making your output better and available as quickly and efficiently as possible is paramount to creating a competitive organization.

Often getting a solution that is 80% of what is desired has a higher ROI than delaying the solution until it is closer to perfect. Be action oriented and keep things moving in the direction that solves the problem at the root and achieves the cited deliverables. Every issue is different and should be considered on its own merit but ponder the pros and cons of following up with the remaining 20% at a future time. Consider the win of prompt issue closure and creating momentum.

Tool - Data

Data may be the geekiest word ever and that's fine. We'll own that. Here's the thing though, --it is numbers, --simply numbers. It has no attachment to opinions, pride or eccentricities. It doesn't care what you think it is, or what you think it should be, it just is what it is. The ultimate in self-confidence. Seek it, learn it, ask it, and let it share its story exactly as it was meant to. Know that hidden inside it are the facts, the truth.

Facts about the process, the system and how the data is collected. Leveraged properly, data is the truth and the truth shall set us free.

Now, if we truly want to understand a system, then we must embrace the concept that the best information is found through quantifiable unbiased data. Unadulterated data, when properly reviewed, takes the guesswork out of the work that needs to be done.

Tool – Process Monitoring

Making a habit of monitoring your data helps distinguish signal to noise. You see all processes have noise. The important thing to know is when there is an actual signal that marks a change. It is for this reason that data should be collected for key processes even if no work is currently planned and especially if it can be collected without impacting someone's time (automation).

For reasons of wasted energy, it can also be argued that collecting data with no intent of using it is wasteful so, again, we default to case by case review and people are our most important assets.

For our purposes, we'll want to monitor our process before, during and after the change is implemented. We should be able to confirm a clear signal that upon implementation, the process output has truly gotten better. Note that once any change is made, we must test the process no matter how confident of the change we may feel. Should the change be incorrect, we'd want to know immediately because bad changes affect our profit and loss statement in the negative direction. Then we'll want to monitor that process over the long term for confirmation of the stability of our process.

Critical Concept - First Pass Yield

Being expeditious with resources means we need an approach that leads to the highest probability of being correct the first time. The concept of first-pass yield is a ratio of how many things we did right to how many things we did the first time we did it. If we created new employee badges 90 times out of 100 correctly than we have a 90% first-pass yield. If we can improve that first pass yield then we are doing this process more efficiently and effectively affecting our P&L positively. It doesn't matter how little you pay someone to perform rework of any type, it will always be cheaper to do it right the first time. This is the essence of our journey.

__Coach's Note:__ Bear with us for a minute as we take that concept one step further. If we have two steps in our process each having a 90% "first pass yield," then the probability of achieving good output through the process becomes 90% x 90% or 81%. Add a few more steps in the process and suddenly 90% "first pass yield" reveals itself as not nearly good enough.

We said we wouldn't get too technical and that was the most technical portion of the book so if you can follow that, then we're all safe.

Tool - Systemic Thinking

Solid foundational thinking when executing good change is to move to the systems approach. Without systems, what are your chances to sustain good change and growth? Consider the method(s) that support the results or output you are intending to affect. Where will real change need to occur in order to create a long term shift toward consistent and accurate results? Everything has a system. Even the lack of a system is a system. Don't be disappointed when the expectations aren't met on an assumed or word of mouth system.

Have you ever told someone that a certain competency was stated during new employee orientation and that they should recall it? Have you ever sat someone in your office and counseled them on a performance issue only to find out they had no idea they were supposed to do that? Is there a system in place that helps them be successful? Were expectations clear?

The bottom line is that if we cannot show employees exactly what excellence looks like then how can we hold them accountable to it?

Creating systems that employees can be successful in is the burden of leadership.

An example of non-system thinking is when a customer makes a complaint after receiving bad output and the response action that occurs is to go back to the group or individual that made the error and tell them they made the mistake. When that's all they do, have they changed the probability that the issue will repeat? That limited 'corrective action' is referred to dismissively (consciously or subconsciously) as training, the need to complete a response for the customer is checked off the 'to do' list and the problem is expected to go away, at least for now, which in short sighted companies, is regarded as good enough. That kind of thinking doesn't affect real change or decrease the long term odds of repeating the escape and duplicating associate recovery costs. It doesn't eliminate the eventual resulting disappointment for the customer. In the end, this type of problem resolution costs more, on so many levels, than fixing it right the first time.

Coach's Note: *Please take note that when training or coaching is the only corrective action for an issue, this is an identifier for the high probability of issue recurrence.*

In case there was any question, this is not the type of "remaining 20%" we were discussing in the "Time to Market" section discussed earlier.

When you consider the costs associated with first delivering poor quality, then secondly responding to the issue with ineffective solutions and then investing resources a third time to correct the corrective action, then as your own CEO, don't you have a duty to sit down with yourself and have a very serious discussion? After all, you're costing your company too much money.

How can any company afford to do things three times? Your Profit and Loss Statement will have red ink (lost revenue) all over it, especially if you allow this type of behavior to continue, or worse, permeate across your organization as acceptable thinking. Do you want to triple your profits or your headaches? Do things right the first time.

No company or individual would ever admit they intended to provide bad quality, however, metrics in many of today's companies are rarely designed to illuminate this type of waste, especially outside of manufacturing. Yet the behavior not only costs money but also conveys a very direct disrespect to your customer.

Applying learning from a systemic perspective enables immediate containment and response for the issue while leveraging action that addresses the real cause, eliminates pain in the form of wasted time, fosters growth and chocks the wheels of progress. Involving others in the improvement process creates improved solutions, team wins, positively impacts morale, perpetuates success and begins that flywheel of momentum turning for long term sustainable growth. Remember, good change starts with us.

Tool – 5 Why?

There is a problem-solving tool called the "5 Why." Essentially it says that at the end of asking "Why?" 5 times you should be at the root cause of any issue and solving for that root cause will ensure you've affected the underlying source of the discrepancy. Well, me, myself, and I like to say that the sixth "Why?" will end up back at management. After all, management is responsible for ensuring robust systems are in place and accountability for the processes we own is a basic function of management.

Critical Concept – Training and Strategies for Learning

There's a theory we like to share with respect to training and presentations. It goes like this; *tell them what you are going to tell them, tell them, and tell them you told them.* We like to take it one step further and add, *then give them something they can refer to later.* Basically, it states that repetition is the key to adult (or any) learning. Studies have demonstrated that most people retain ten percent of what we see, thirty to forty percent of what we see and hear, and ninety percent of what we see, hear and do. These percentages degrade with time so providing a reference for the student allows them to access it when the time comes for actual use.

Going this distance means you're on the road to making expectations clear. Anything short of that is not setting up your customer, the recipient of the training, for success.

Tool – Process Flow Diagram

Imagine that we've narrowed our focus to a specific initiative. Improvement begins with a truthful understanding of where we are. Seeking the truth requires unbiased insight. This is a key concept to mature problem-solving. What this means is that in order for us to enable ourselves to recognize the truth, we must unlearn what we think we know.

Begin by breaking the process into its individual steps. In order to truly affect good-change, we have to consider the whole system that supports the initiative we will work on. Think through the suppliers of the inputs to the process and the recipients of the output of the process to ensure consideration of all perspectives. Now let's map out the steps in our process by creating a flow diagram.

Simply stated a flow diagram is a pictorial representation of the process. It shows the order and direction of operations using specific shapes to denote the type of step. Leverage the symbols in the table below and draw your process flow diagram also known as the process map. The symbols are relatively self-explanatory but a brief description is included. Note that creating the process flow diagram in a team ensures all folks engaged in the change are on the same page, literally, with respect to the process. This discussion and the resulting unified understanding of the process is such an important part of the improvement process. This point cannot be overstated and the true process learning becomes a focal point of celebration at the end of the project. Begin with the end in mind and take the time needed to create a proper process map.

Establishing the right level of detail in your map can be tricky. The key is to be at the right level to observe improvement opportunities without getting mired in the weeds. Think iteratively, coming back to steps and breaking them into the next level of detail is easy when compared against spending an hour discussing the first step in the process. Because of the iterative nature of the approach, it is often beneficial to use sticky notes to write steps down and post on the wall. Steps can easily be rearranged in their order, broken into smaller pieces and more. Flexibility is key to getting to the appropriate resulting process map. Especially the first time it is done. When a team creates the flow diagram it quickly becomes evident that no individual knows every step in the process. It can also become apparent that there are misunderstandings and pitfalls that need clarity or improved approaches. The collaborative method yields better results because of diverse perspectives. Capture inevitable improvement ideas in a bin list as you progress and keep the focus on creating the flow diagram. When the team begins their focus on creating the improved process, be sure and share the collections of improvement ideas captured in the bin lists.

Table 1 – Process Mapping Symbols

Symbol	Meaning
	Terminator – This symbol marks the beginning or end of your process. Because it marks the beginning or end, the terminator can only have one input or output, not both. Terminators clearly denote the boundary of the process. Often there is significant confusion over boundaries and clarity here can eliminate confusion and deter waste in your process.
	Activity – Use this symbol and a few keywords inside it to describe a step in the process. Note that the arrows depict the direction of flow.

⬦ (decision diamond)	**Decision** – This symbol states that a decision is made and that a single input will need a determination of two possible outcomes.
● (circle)	**Inspection** – An inspection is considered waste because it takes resources and adds no value to transforming the part or service provided. It is colored red as a visual aid to assist in spotting waste.
⌓ (D-shape)	**Delay** - A delay is considered waste because it ties up resources and adds no value to transforming the part or service provided. It is colored red as a visual aid to assist in spotting waste.
→	**Connector** – Used to show the connection of steps as well as the direction of flow of those steps.
ANSI: Note that the symbols demonstrated here come from the American National Standard Institute (ANSI) created to help drive a common language. There are many symbols that provide more detail however these symbols are good enough for our purposes.	

There are rules for flowcharting and these too can get detailed. Let's keep the following in mind. The process starts with a terminator. Label the beginning terminator with the word 'Start'. An arrow (connector) should emerge from the terminator and move to the first step of the process. Interesting considerations here include clarity around the process boundary. Are we sure that is the first step? Would the upstream supplier agree? Do we have our expectations clearly stated for our supplier to help them understand what success looks like? In fact, is the upstream supplier included in the group and able to accurately portray their deliverables? Do those deliverables agree with your expectations?

<u>Activities</u> have an input and an output? We should consider if each of the activities in the process are well understood? If they have consistent and accurate output? If they are the constraint for the process? The constraint is the longest step (activity) in a series of steps that inhibit progress toward its goal. Every process has a constraint. Some constraints make a direct impact on our P&L in that if more products or services were able to get through the constraint, the company would enjoy increased revenue. The constraint is often referred to as the bottleneck. Understanding where the constraint is located is critical to improvement and we'll color it yellow so that we are reminded of its location and importance. The theory of constraints is a significant science. For our purposes, we want to know where it is and consider what we can do to support and improve flow through the constraint.

<u>Coach's Note:</u> If you want to gain alliances with manufacturing, ask them where the constraint is and what you can do to help support it. Their answer may be as simple as naming the step and asking that anytime one of the employees from the constraint asks for support, you give them priority so they can quickly return to running the constraint. By definition, revenue lost at the constraint cannot be recovered and that affects everyone.

Decisions represent the fork in the road where the process can go this way or that. What decisions will need to be made? Are those decisions clearly demarcated enabling fast, accurate and consistent flow?

Coach's Note: *If you are walking through this process by yourself, don't skip this step of creating the process flow diagram. The process map is a powerful tool for holistic process thinking and will positively impact the results of your effort. You are encouraged to leverage the tool and look for opportunities to use in team settings where you will be surprised to discover the difference between what people think is well understood and what is actually well understood.*

Critical Concept - No System is Perfect

If you've walked through the exercise of completing your process map, the next thing we need to do is acknowledge that all systems have some amount of waste. Yes, even the ones that we may own. At some point, it may become cost-prohibitive to remove more waste from a process however that is rarely the case. Identifying and removing waste leads to more efficient and effective systems ultimately giving time back to you.

Tool - Learning to See Waste

Learning to see waste is a critical skill. It sounds simple and actually, it really is, but let's just humor the process and walk through a brief overview of the "Seven (plus two) Deadly Wastes". These wastes include; defects, over-production, transportation, waiting, inventory, motion, and excess processing. There are two more wastes that we like to share, the waste of power and the worst, the waste of intellectual capital. Keep in mind that the words that make up the acronym were created in a manufacturing environment and *lean* a little in that direction (do you suppose that's why it's called Lean?). We'll keep the names in hopes of aligning common language within your origination and we'll provide examples to assist the transition to the HR world.

The 7.2 Deadly Wastes

Defects – Perhaps the most self-descriptive of wastes, a defect is a shortcoming or a noncompliance relative to established expectations (e.g. the Purchase Order contract with the client) and simply doing something wrong is a waste. Defective output must either be disposed of and recreated or reworked into compliance. Sometimes in service organizations, defects are worse than in production environments. For example, creating a bad paycheck cannot simply be thrown in the garbage, forgotten and written off at tax time. A bad paycheck has to be resolved. Imagine if the error was not noticed for several pay periods, for several employees or the entire organization. Again, doing things right the first time is always the lowest cost approach.

Following the bad paycheck example, consider how we might address the discrepancy to ensure it never, ever, happens again. When we're correcting the system that produced the bad paychecks, we'd start by asking why it happened. The first time we ask why we might determine that our payroll company produced bad checks. The second time we ask why we might determine that our payroll company received bad input from our company. Generally speaking, by the time we ask the fifth why we should be at the root cause of the issue. Affecting the root cause with a robust solution will decrease or eliminate the possibility of recurrence. That's making real change, good change. When this approach permeates an organization and becomes a part of the culture, customers notice, suppliers and competitors will notice. They'll start to make requests for benchmarking opportunities to figure out how you do what you do. Competitors will refer to yours as world-class. The interesting thing is that the people do not have to change, not necessarily, the mindset does. Imagine a world where your company's excellent reputation is your chief marketing tool.

Note that if we ask one more "why?" in the example above, we come back to management. Management is responsible for setting up the workforce to be successful. Management commitment means accepting that responsibility and resourcing appropriately to build robust systems that produce good stuff, on time, every time.

Over-processing – Simply put, this is doing more than what is required. Inspection although sometimes necessary because the risk of passing on bad material may be more expensive then inspecting it out. Inspection steps are very often created out of a response to something that went wrong. The danger here is that the inspection becomes the norm. Instead, we should look to reduce or eliminate inspections as our confidence in the strength of our process grows quantifiably. Challenge the inspection steps. What did they originate from? Are they really needed?

Transportation – This waste refers to large scale movements like traveling from one plant to another to roll out a new policy. Consider the risks versus rewards. There are other options that exist that can reduce or eliminate the need for transportation. In the process of brainstorming alternatives, we may determine that the value of sharing in a face to face forum is critical and we might choose to forgo the video conference. The action of considerate brainstorming may led to the idea of videotaping for the inevitable few who cannot attend due to the ever-present competing priorities. This solution saves us from the personal cost of one on one training after bulk deployment. Considering the return on investment. Videotaping may be an acceptable and lowest cost approach.

Waiting – Anytime there is a situation where, in order to complete the activity, one must wait for another activity to complete is an example of waiting waste. Consider that the deployment of a new policy requires the CEO's signature but the CEO has been tied up with other matters. Simply waiting outside his/her door for the last-minute signature is an example of waiting waste.

Take the CEO's signature a step further. When he or she finally has the opportunity to review and sign-off it causes a lot of last-minute scrambling and schedule recovery. Perhaps the roll-out meeting has to be rescheduled (synonymous with defect waste (rework)). The effort that went into booking the room, the individuals, etc. is also rework waste, then some people didn't immediately get the cancellation and showed up. All of these things are waste because of waiting for that signature. The bottom line, is the signature really necessary? Was that really why the CEO wanted to sign? Are they aware of the waste and what alternatives exist? Certainly, there's a better answer somewhere.

The signature may have been the first solution that came up when discussing the risks of deployment of the policy without the CEO's formal approval. Consider what would have been the second, best answer? Meaning, if the team brainstormed a bit longer, what other ideas would have come up. After generating the next best answers we start to recognize a hierarchy born out of our creativity. Eventually, the best answer rises to the top. Sometimes it's the first answer but more often than not it's the pursuit of the next best ideas that leads to breakthrough thinking.

Coach's Note: *Ideas are like musical notes, having one is not enough. You need to have several to know if you've got a worthwhile arrangement.*

Inventory – Often, excess inventory is created to buffer, hide or accommodate for weaknesses in the system that produce the output. An example might be to purchase extra books for a specific training because you don't believe the managers took an accurate count of who would be required to participate. Perhaps the excess is justified to future training but a lean organization drives the behavior of getting exactly what is needed exactly when it is needed. Anything else is considered waste. Inventory is only good if it's sold. Have you ever purchased a certain office supply only to watch it sit on the shelf because the person that asked for it was the only person that wanted it but it came with a minimum order quantity? These are examples of inventory waste.

Coach's Note: *Curiosity is such a powerful tool. Asking the "what if...?" question relative to the office supply issue might lead us to a new perspective. Have you ever seen an office supply cabinet cluttered with stuff nobody seems to want? Is that causing people to have to search longer than necessary for what they do need? After all, they are supposed to be working, not shopping.*

Hey, what if we dated all the inventory in the office supply cabinet when it came in? What could we learn, how could that affect the work we do, the money we spend, the way we store the supplies?

Have you ever seen the office supplies behind the Fort Knox level security cage complete with the need for perfectly completed paperwork? That's how we turn a need for a AAA battery into a half-day trek through the wilderness of the Bureaucratic Canyons of Mount Save-A-Penny. This highly defensible armory complete with security cameras and the distrusting guard sneering at your obviously phony story of needing to get your mouse running again. WHAT IF that dead mouse occurred not at a time of the users choosing? What could it be delaying them from doing while they WAIT for their now $40 battery? Maybe a sales proposal to a key client expecting it by 4:00pm?

What if everyone got extra batteries when they don't need them out of paranoia of lost time when they do?

Ahhhh batteries, hidden are your true costs, you sly little devil. Safety glasses too.

Think about it. The same insurance that pays if you get hurt at work pays if you get hurt at home. Take the safety glasses home, take two!

Motion – Transportation is often considered at the macro-level while motion is at the micro-level. The goal being to minimize motion (e.g. footsteps). Leverage the concept and apply it creatively. Being customer-centric, you might consider how many clicks a customer must go through to find the information they are looking for on your internet page. By reducing clicks, you've reduced their effort and that would be analogous to waste of motion. Laying out your work area in a way that puts items used regularly throughout the day within reach, items used once a day in your drawer and a few times a week in the nearby cabinet is an example of reducing waste associated with motion.

Processing (excess) – Have you ever seen a policy go through a large number of people for approval when all that should have seen it is at most one representative from each of the perspectives that needed to review it? That's probably enough said on this topic but let's take it the inevitable step further. Often it leads to over-analysis, discussion, excessive wordsmithing, and other unnecessary delays. Better to have a solid representation from each perspective and have them take the effort seriously. Dare I say that holiday display committees can stimulate so much discussion about perspectives and feelings that in the end, the decision may get made to forgo the effort? Some might say, "It's just not worth it." It's synonymous with over-engineering.

In the end, the very thing that the company was trying to do to keep the personal touch and team spirit ends up causing stress. The stress seems to directly correlate to the number of people involved in making the decoration decisions. Often the stress is caused by invented perspectives.

In general, a little correlation between the calendar and the entrance(s) to the building is well perceived by most. We're probably getting into the borderlands of controversial topics. Our goal is more to illicit the application of the concepts rather than to get controversial. We wish you the happiest of holidays whatever that means for you personally.

Plus Two - The seven wastes described above are common. The two that often get missed are:

Intellectual Capital – Perhaps the greatest sin of waste is not harnessing the people around you for their knowledge, their desire to creatively solve problems and make their impact on the organization. Very simply put, your organization is teaming (pun intended) with knowledge from a diverse set of perspectives (the ultimate definition of diversity). Leveraging the people for their ideas about how to improve the process they work in is often the fastest way to improve the process.

By the way, you never know where the next best answer will come from. It might be the innovation engineer or it might be the custodial engineer. Why not create an environment where people feel safe to share their ideas for improvement. Not only will it help lead to great solutions but there's a 'feel-good' part of seeing your ideas implemented and morale is a critical part of any team's growth. Integrating people into the wins of the organization is a crucial part of building momentum toward pride and success. People love to be a part of a winning team, especially when they are a key part of those wins. The organization chart should convey the concept of what position on the team each employee represents and plays. It shouldn't be construed as being the hierarchy of, or provide a locator for, the best or only idea generator(s).

***Coach's Note on Brainstorming** – A brainstorming session is a great way to harness the power of a team in generating ideas. A few things to keep in mind is to guide the team with an objective and then not stifle output. Filtering will come later and creating an environment of free/creative thinking and building on ideas is important in the early brainstorming phase. After all, many world-class solutions started out with a single, crazy idea.*

Equipment & Energy – The waste of equipment refers to the availability of machinery in the broad sense. For example, having the printer down prior to a training session where you want the attendees to have a hard copy so they can make notes creates waste for lack of equipment availability.

The waste of energy refers to power being left on where power is not needed. In the current day, these types of wastes are decreasing in impact due to technology like motion sensors that shut lights off in areas where not in use. LEDs are so much more efficient than incandescent lights but that doesn't mean we should ignore it. In fact, is your thermostat programmable and properly programmed? Is it set to the right time (e.g. daylight savings)? There is no sense in having it set to a comfortable level outside of the times when the area is in use. Does the laminator need to plug into a timed outlet because people often seem to forget to turn it off? More than just an energy waste, that's a safety concern. You get the idea.

The acronym DOTWIMPIE helps us remember the different types of wastes but more important than categorizing waste is the ability to recognize it. Keep in mind that these are examples used to illicit application of the concepts to your world. People are any company's most valuable assets and that includes you. Shape these concepts to fit what waste looks like in your specific situation and work to eliminate it.

In regard to our process, let's pause for a moment and share a word on customers. Everything we do must align with our customers. That's the part in our strategy that states how we make money. Depending on the scenario, there are at least 3 (if not 4) customers to every process; there's the downstream recipient of our output often referred to as the internal customer. There's the end-user of the output, often referred to as the end customer. Sometimes there is a bulk purchaser of our output making a third customer.

For example, the employee is the end-user of the paycheck and your company is the bulk buyer of paychecks. The payroll company would be foolish to design their solution only to achieve what the employee states as their requirements. We must consider all our customers in an effort to build the right solutions and properly fuel our financial engine.

There is fourth customer however, that is almost never mentioned or considered. That customer is each other. We all may hold different positions in our organizations and at different levels but from the overarching perspective, we all play our part. We owe it to each other to know our position and play it well.

To bring this point home, imagine a dirty bathroom that employees from maintenance use, then one inevitable day, you're providing a tour to a client and they ask to use the restroom. Instantaneously you realize how dirty and outdated that restroom is. Attempting to avoid the embarrassment you try to talk the client into using the restroom in the front office area. Humbly, and urgently, they decline and use the closest one. At that moment, we realize several opportunities for learning, not the least of which is customers are potty trained. That they use bathrooms and not always at the time of our choosing. We recognize that we have slighted our maintenance crew of the restroom they deserve despite the particulars of the cleanliness of the work they do. Often, this simple thing can be the brick and mortar that builds the wall of "us" versus "them." Such an unhealthy thought to allow to infiltrate the organization.

What if there was a wash sink design that was specific for dirty jobs and easy cleanup? How far would that go in making our maintenance crew feel valued like a critical part of the team?

Tool - Risk Mitigation

Managing risk is a concept that has been around for many years (ask any insurance company) however ISO and other industry certifications are starting to increase awareness of the topic. Regarding risk, we must be aware of three critical components relative to each potential failure type; the potential size of the impact, the rate of recurrence, and the relative ease of being able to notice when it goes wrong. If the impact is large, like in the paycheck example, and potential for occurrence is high (it just happened), and we have low potential to detect the discrepancy (it got through to our customer) then in order to protect ourselves from repeat, we may need implement some sort of check to help us be successful. Note that any check (no pun intended) we put in place will require resources. Since the check does not actually assist in creating the output, it affects our overhead and costs us money while adding no value. That's a negative impact on our P&L and although it may be necessary in the short term, our long term goal would be to eliminate the non-value added check with appropriate confidence to lean out the process and reduce associate costs. We should always be looking to reduce or eliminate inspection steps in an effort to reduce our costs but never at the expense of escapes to our customer(s).

Tool – 5S

5S is a popular Lean tool you have likely already heard of. We'll provide a high-level introduction here as many companies have training available. Some call the system 6S with the sixth S referred to as safety however safety is a critical aspect of the entire 5S system so rather than treating it separately, we prefer to integrate the concept across each of the 5S'. The steps are listed in order and represent a flow of steps in 5S'ing an area.

1S - Sort – Sort is the first step and refers to removing all unneeded items in an area. Simply reducing or eliminating clutter makes it easier to find items and makes the area safer.

2S - Set in Order – This step ensures that there is a place for everything and everything is in its place. Consider the activities of the target work area. How does the system flow and in what order? The area should be laid out such that it embraces the flow, not fights with it.

3S - Shine – Shine is a straight forward concept. It refers to making everything look pristine such that issues can be spotted immediately. Some companies will paint all their equipment white in this step to assist in making issues (e.g. leaky equipment) immediately apparent.

Regardless of the avenue you take, now that you've removed all dirt and grime, keep it that way.

4S - Standardize - Create a common system and establish expectations regarding use, storage, replenishment, etc. as appropriate. Create pride for the area and share the responsibility of keeping it clean and uncluttered. Post pictures of how the area is expected to look and assign appropriate ownership to take charge of keeping it that way. Note that doesn't mean taking the responsibility away from the people that use the area.

5S - Sustain - Commitment to following the system on a daily basis. Well known to be the hardest of the 5S' and the most important. Set expectations and post a schedule with a checklist to drive accountability and recognize the effort that demonstrates the right behavior. It takes 21 days to create a new behavior. After that, its second nature and just happens.

Tool - Waste Walk

A waste walk is an end to end walk through your process with a singular focus of looking for the 7.2 Deadly Wastes. Make this as physical as possible and literally follow the steps for the process you have in mind. If your process occurs online and interacts with other competencies, then go and visit the people that interact in the process.

Tell them you are running a test and interview them for their piece, how it works, concerns or snags they may have, etc. Help them understand what you are trying to do and assure them that you want to be a good supplier in the process. Do they have any feedback? How would things work better? Could we walk through it together?

You might not be able to fix everything and you might even have to leverage the scope of the project from your charter document but this singular effort begins the snowball effect gathering momentum toward a better company where work is smarter, not harder.

For example, consider how your public files are set up. Can you easily find what you need to? Now the real question, can your customers? How many, "Can you tell me where I can find this or that?" questions do you get? What are the demographics of people that ask? Is it just the new folks? Does that indicate an issue with logic (veterans can find because of memory, not logic)? What other processes do you own/support? Are they effective, efficient? Create a bin list for improvement ideas and have them available for the future.

Tool – Bin List

A bin list of ideas is a pretty simple tool and can be very powerful for continuing progress. As ideas come up, capture them in the bin list so that effort can continue along the lines it was going when the idea came up. Rather than shifting to a new line of thinking, it allows progress to continue and acknowledges that the idea is captured for detailed discussion at a future time.

Critical Concept - Avoid Assumptions

Human nature is hardwired to quickly get to problem-solving. After reading the previous questions relative to publicly shared files did you jump to considering working on something you'd been meaning to do for a long time? Those words prompted you to think of opportunity as well as action. That's good but let's embrace the improvement process with a little more rigor in the form of quantifiable information (data) and leverage a stronger way of determining where to put our limited and precious energy first. Making assumptions and jumping straight to problem-solving is a common pitfall. Avoid the trap.

A good way to think about how to prioritize what should be worked on is to consider the impact on our resources. When we talk about wasteful impact on resources, we like to refer to it as pain and since time really is money, virtually all pain can be quantified in terms of money. Those sources of pain are wounds that bleed red ink all over our P&L statement. Learn to locate the origin of the pain (root cause) and stop the bleeding. Drive resolution at the source and optimize profits. People that can speak to and impact profit and loss are more valuable to companies. Traditionally, people that add more value make more money.

Again, there is good news because if we can measure it, we can manage it. If we can manage it, we can improve it. If we can improve it, we can make it world class. World-class companies traditionally have longer lifespans, reap optimized profits, value their employees, have higher employee morale, better total compensation and less turnover than lesser performing companies. Those kinds of companies sound like a pretty good place to be.

Note that world-class performance does not directly translate to large multinational corporations. Small and midsize companies can have world-class performance too. To continue, higher employee morale begets higher employee engagement which is tantamount to holistic continuous improvement perpetuating the cycle and increasing overall job satisfaction as well as profitability. Harnessing the intellectual capital of the organization creates the best solution time and time again. If you have heard of the Toyota Production System, this concept is at the core.

Coach's Note: Whoa, sorry, perhaps we geeked out a bit there. As much as we truly believe in the concepts here, let's reel things in a bit and start with something we can all relate to, -ourselves. If you recall *from the training discussion, we retain 90% of what we see, hear, and do. Shortly and together, we will begin a project for hands-on learning.*

Note that our approach can be modified to impact at any level of the organization and we're not talking about rocket surgery so if we just start with a personal project, we'll learn the system and have the confidence to expand for larger impacts.

When we are ready to select our first project, it might be okay to filter your scope to stay within a process well in your control. This will ensure you are empowered to quickly and easily implement change and affect the output of the process while you learn/gain comfort with this problem-solving approach. Keep in mind, however, that filtering hides reality and may limit you from affecting the biggest opportunity for gain. Further, if you are targeting a process with shared ownership, taking it on as a solo project could backfire with tremendous backlash.

We know the HR professional can relate to the concept that job satisfaction comes in two types; personal and team. Out of selfishness as well as stacking the deck in our favor, we'll focus mostly on the personal first with the understanding that we can then expand these concepts to improve team satisfaction as well.

Critical Concept – Test and Measure

This concept is another simple yet powerful one. Before we completely deploy any change or system, we'll run it in a pilot first testing it to see if we've missed anything. We'll measure its output and determine if any modifications are necessary. This concept makes no assumptions and acknowledges the fact that *'we don't know what we don't know.'* That a little due diligence can help us avoid making costly mistakes. There is no shame in making mistakes but we should do what we can to minimize their impact.

Chapter 3 – Applied Learning

Up until now, we've discussed a lot of theory relative to good change and solid decision making. Now that we've laid the foundation for why good change makes sense and provided some education on specific tools that are available, let's get into the nuts and bolts of how to flow through making good change. Since there is no substitute for experience, let's do this project together. The following is a step by step approach to a real-world yet hypothetical improvement project. Please mirror the steps in your real world and you will be the recipient of your effort.

Our Mission

Our Mission, should we decide to accept it, is to give ourselves the gift of time. Let's bring these thoughts closer to something near and dear to us, -us.

In order to embrace the concepts being presented, let's think selfishly for a moment. How much time do you waste because interruptions throw you off the momentum you had going on a certain project or task? If you are like most HR professionals, interruptions are the norm. In fact, for some, the whole day is an interruption and any movement toward completing something on our "to-do list" is a bonus. Don't get us wrong, from an HR professional perspective we want engagement however we can all agree that some types of interruptions are more valuable than others.

Hey, acknowledging the truth can be difficult but working in an imaginary reality doesn't do anyone any favors, not in this fable. Think about it, solving a problem that isn't a priority or real (even worse) is wasting more time you already don't have enough of. Confrontation of a problem done constructively, and with an open mind, is a first-step toward resolution. That is a critical component of the rise to high-performance teams. Resolution sounds a lot like an improvement. If we can prioritize the right improvements than we are on our way to a better tomorrow.

Step 1 - Align with our Strategy.

Recall our strategy discussion, we always want to connect what we do to our corporate strategy. Let's assume, that one of the initiatives in our corporate strategy is to improve customer satisfaction. We'll call it Strategic Objective Number One (SO1). Keep in mind that the HR organization has at least an internal and an external customer base. For clarity through demonstration, we will walk through a process that will be mutually beneficial to our internal customers and ourselves. This will support SO1 and there is no shame in making our lives a little easier as we make things more effective for our internal customers. That's the very definition of a win-win solution.

Step 2 - Prioritize Focus

In this step, we're going to generate some data to demonstrate how to create it when none exits but our long term goal will be to have data for key processes being gathered all the time. Data gathered in the background for eventual analysis is referred to as passive data collection. Data that you intentionally gather for a specific effort is referred to as active data collection.

This step will be a little awkward the first time because we need data but we haven't created it yet. In real life, once we have data relative to our key processes in the format that we will illustrate shortly, then we'll have it for all our needs moving forward. Essentially, from this point forward, we'll be plucking the next project off our data-driven improvement queue tree. Therefore, the data we need to justify our action will already be available and lead is to the correct next priority to work on.

For now, let's take that selfish perspective we mentioned previously. That every time someone interrupts us with a question and the answer is already available to them via the intranet or other support systems, that it is waste of time for that person (our customer) and for ourselves.

After all, they have to go out of their way in their busy day to ask the HR organization a question and we have to navigate the interruption and allocate time to respond. This perspective may seem harsh but ask yourself, "If I really care about my customers, take ownership of my process, and run my business like I am the CEO, then doesn't it represent a defect, need additional resources in the form of rework and represent the truth?" After all, if the information is available to the company, then having to ask someone for help to find it means that something is interfering with them getting to it on their own. This initiative aligns well with our corporate-wide strategic object, "Improve Customer Satisfaction" also known as SO1.

We need a way to quantify the interruptions and understand where we are feeling the most pain. Since no system exists currently to gather that information, let's create one. After a few minutes of thinking things through, we came to the conclusion that the following is a pretty solid first pass at a data collection system that will help us understand the truth relative to our interruption opportunity. This is the output of the team and each of the categories is defined as follows.

1) **Benefits** – For tracking questions relative to employee benefits that are, or should be, available to them.

2) **Events** - For tracking questions relative to planned events like business update meetings, recruiting events, and company functions that are available as common knowledge.

3) **Onboarding** – Questions that come from new employees like where is the mailroom, how do I get my new badge and the like. These questions have answers which had already been explained and are available to the employees.

4) **Payroll** – Questions or changes relative to payroll, time tracking and time clock usage.

5) **Relations** – Questions relative to managing standard employee relations like reviews, complaints, corrective action plans, and the like.

6) **Customer or Supplier Visits** – Questions and support relative to customer or supplier visits. They are categorized together since each have the similar support requirements.

7) **Other** – Includes items like terminations that don't currently happen on a scale large enough to warrant their own category. This will also serve as a 'catch-all' category.

As you apply the concepts and capture your own data, it will be apparent that your system may need tweaking and that's fine. Lock it in as soon as you can and then hold it fast.

It is urged to have a category called 'Other' because some issues will come up that just don't fit in any of the defined buckets and being forced to place them in the wrong category is a form of data manipulation (more on that shortly). The 'Other' bucket should end up with the least amount of items in it. As you make good change however, the 'Other' category will eventually benefit from a proper break down into its appropriate categories continuing the cycle of improvement.

Adding elements of time and other items led us to the following data collection sheet. Every time we get a question, we fill out the relatively self-descriptive information as appropriate.

Interruption Data Collection System

Date	Category	Sub Category	Quantification of Impact (hours)	Origin	Description/Notes	Week
12/24/2019	Onboarding	Resource Search	2.6	Production	Where is the guard shack?	12/28/2019
12/23/2019	Supplier Visit	Preparation	2.2	Production	Robert requesting update to submitted hours for Larry	12/28/2019
12/23/2019	Payroll	Change Request	5.7	Production	Robert requesting update to submitted hours for Edith	12/28/2019
12/18/2019	Onboarding	Resource Search	2.6	Production	Where is the guard shack?	12/21/2019
12/16/2019	Payroll	Change Request	5.2	Production	Robert requesting update to submitted hours for Cassandra	12/21/2019
12/9/2019	Payroll	Change Request	4.9	Production	Robert requesting update to submitted hours for Cora	12/14/2019

Of course, it makes sense to track the date of the interruption, the length of time of the interruption, and the relevant category or topic of the interruption. Less obvious data collection topics include; sub-category, the origin of the interruption and notes relative to the interruption. Often, these next level of detail items come as a response to testing the first data collections system and determining that it wasn't providing enough information (Test and Measure). We learned from the first generation data collection system and made an iteration to something better.

Note that a subcategory column was added because often that next level of detail can assist in understanding the issues and therefore the solutions. The data is truncated here and represents a portion of our data collected to date. All data is used to create the graphs you will see in the analysis phase. As you work on this project, consider your next projects in the queue and begin collecting data appropriately for them. Keep in mind that making no assumptions is the golden rule for good problem-solving.

Coach's Note: *Over the years, we've learned to test our measurement system before fully deploying it. Often it can have flaws in it like an inability to measure accurately or have the capability to be reproducible one person to the next. Another lesson we've learned is to represent data by week. It lends itself to telling the better story. Always capture the date (and time if appropriate) but summarizing and graphing by week is less noisy than by day and more response-able than by month over the longer term.*

A note on notes. Adding the column of notes allows us to capture information that may become relevant over time though may not be immediately apparent. It could provide information that helps us determine the root cause or another category we need to comprehend. We make it a habit to always add a field for free form text notes.

Now let's suppose that we've been leveraging our data collection system and collecting information for several weeks. We just completed a deployment of a new benefits provider and suddenly have a little break in the action to move to the next step in our SO1 focused Interruption Initiative. We decide to take a closer look at the data and ask it what story it is trying to tell us. Here's what we find.

Graph I: Interruption Impact Histogram

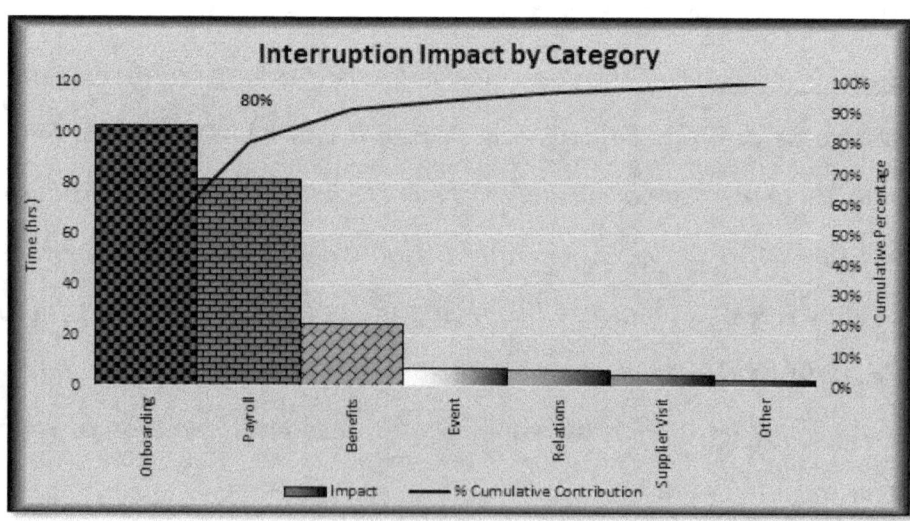

Graph II: Interruption Impact Trend

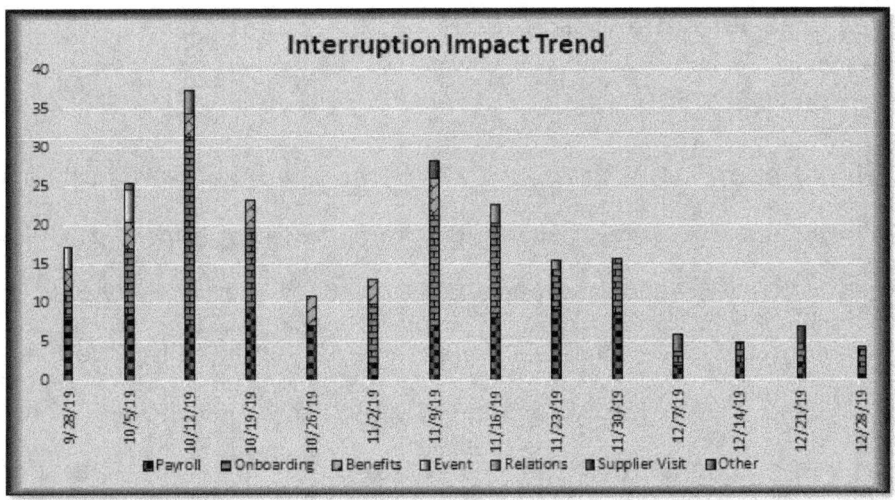

In this illustration, you will note that the two biggest categories in the histogram are "Onboarding" and "Payroll" respectively. This sometimes aligns with what you were thinking but more often can provide unexpected results and expanded knowledge. For example, you might recall that it wasn't long ago that issues regarding 'Benefits' were much higher. The recent change in providers worked out really well.

We've got our focus narrowed down to two processes; Onboarding and Payroll. It is quite evident from that "Interruption Impact by Category" Pareto that working on one of those two processes will give us the biggest return on investment. It aligns with our thoughts and we can confirm that these issues are still prevalent with our "Interruption Impact Trend" observed previously. Now, in order to assist our decision making prowess, let's introduce another tool.

Step 3 – Prioritize Project Focus

Tool – Decision Matrix

In the above data example, it was determined that On-Boarding and Payroll were the biggest contributors to our interruptions. Logic would dictate that since Onboarding is the bigger issue, that we should take that on first. Data analytics are great but be reminded that people are always our greatest asset and choosing which project to work on has many interactions other than what this data can tell us. Resources, costs, corporate goals, current events and other things all interact. One tool that can help navigate these turbulent waters is called a decision, project prioritization, or a cause and effect matrix. A decision matrix allows us to acknowledge those interactions and enables us to dynamically quantify which project would be the best one to prioritize for our organization currently.

In this case, we'll use a decision matrix to list potential projects we could take on to affect the pain we are feeling relative to our two top sources of pain and then consider them against a set of criteria. Our end goal is to get the right project to present itself as the most ideal to pursue now given our current circumstances. Essentially, it establishes a set of key decision-making criteria, defines their scoring and weights them prior to any decision making. The goal is that by doing this ahead of time you are creating an unbiased and quantified way to assist in driving the best ideas to pursue to the top of the list.

For example, considerations might include; cost of implementation, ease of implementation, availability of appropriate resources, and impact on the desired outcome. Establishing the scoring criteria might state that anything that costs less than $5,000 to implement might be considered cheap and we'll score that a 9 (note: we'll use a scale of 1, 3, or 9 only and keep the discussion fast and simple). Between 5 and $15,000 would achieve a 3 and more than $15,000 yields a 1. Assign a defined scoring system to your other criteria and then multiply the results together. Then sort the ideas from high score to lowest score to gain perspective on what this approach says is the right place to start. Note that this system is an aid for quantification and no substitute for what we people know. In fact, there may a category referred to as a showstopper. If the idea doesn't have a certain ingredient, it cannot be pursued no matter what the overall score looks like. For example, perhaps a critical expert won't be available for the next 6 months. By definition, we won't be able to pursue projects needing that expert for at least 6 months.

The table below demonstrates a decision-making matrix. It is another simple and powerful decision-making tool keeping bias and personalities out of the proverbial equation.

Table 3 – The Decision Matrix

		Decision Matrix									
	Weight	20%	20%	20%	10%	10%	10%	5%	5%	NA	100%
Project Number	Project Description	Alignment to Strategic Objectives	Ease of Implementation	Associated Costs	Resource Availability	Business Imperitive	Return on Investment	Time to Implementation	Not Used	Show Stopper	Total
1	Onboarding 5S and Safety Training	9	3	3	3	1	1	3	1	NA	370
2	Onboarding Software Training	3	3	9	1	1	1	1	1	NA	340
3	Onboarding Survival Training	3	1	1	3	1	1	3	1	NA	170
4	Payroll and Time Card	9	9	9	3	3	9	9	1	NA	740
5	Benefits FAQ Sheet	3	1	1	1	3	1	1	1	X	160
6	Benefits Provider Change	9	1	1	9	9	9	1	1	NA	500
7	Supplier Feedback Project	3	3	9	3	1	3	1	1	NA	380
8	Event Planning System	3	3	3	1	1	1	1	1	X	220

Coach's Note: The calculation used to achieve each total score is 100 x [Filter Criteria 1 Score x Weight 1 + Filter Criteria 2 Score x Weight 2 + Filter Criteria 3...]) step. The possible scores achievable are a 1, 3, or 9 which is intended to minimize discussion and provide a rapid priority.

From this example, it looks like the 'Payroll and Time Card' project scored the best and will have the highest likelihood of achieving the right results given the weighting and scoring criteria. With the size and scope of the project, more than one project might be pursued given multiple resources. At some time, however, most teams run out of resources and that's okay. Knowing where the line between active and future projects gets drawn builds trust in the team. We simply cannot do everything but we can create a queue and when resources become free, they can take the next project in the queue. Leveraging this approach achieves healthy utilization of resources in an effort to create the largest impact. It keeps work challenging, avoids the flavor of the day and sets a course for improvement.

In the example Decision Matrix provided, eight criteria are shown however one criterion column was not used and that's okay. Leveraging these tools should be kept simple and adapt to your needs. It should not steamroll logic or be manipulated to distort the truth. Make sure your weight percentage sums to one hundred percent, include a column to identify any showstopper(s) and make sure they are considered project by project.

It is possible that the use of a decision matrix is not necessary, perhaps the fast approach implements as many ideas as possible in the timeframe available and that the team feels that's best in this case. That's okay, there are times to be flexible and this may be one of them. However, if you see the team struggling to agree on which action(s) to take on, this tool can be quickly explained and utilized to keep things moving. Again, it can be interesting to see a project float to the top based on its own merits and is a good reminder to leverage quantification when making decisions. Many times a project will become the lead opportunity right in front of the team's eyes though the focus was elsewhere prior to leveraging the tool. Further, the whole team aligns with the logic and agrees that it's the correct project to pursue. For the most part, the team can usually create and score each criterion in real-time but sometimes a little investigation provides background information that helped filter all the potential projects and recognizes the right one to resource now.

Hands-on familiarity with our process and data provides insight. For example, capturing the sub-categories of information we did in our data collections system allowed us to filter our data for just the issues that affected the category of Payroll. We could notice that the majority of corrections were coming from the production floor. A brief discussion with individuals on the floor, their supervisors and managers uncovered a misunderstanding between the production organization and our payroll process. Leveraging that information into the decision-making matrix yielded the 'Payroll and Time Card' project as the number one item to work on as long as the Information Technology (IT) team agreed that there were no showstoppers relative to implementing the anticipated changes needed into the web-based time clock tool.

In our hypothetical example, Ms. Melody championed the effort and made her first priority a quick confirmation with the IT group. Armed with agreement from IT, Ms. Melody pulled her project team kickoff meeting together. Discussions there firmed up hunches and a chartering document was created. The kickoff meeting confirmed that the primary issue here had more to do with misunderstandings than the Payroll and Time Card system itself. The team consisting of 3 key perspectives (Operations, Payroll, and IT) listed out the deliverables that need to be completed, their ownership and associated timelines. The team each worked on their deliverables and in parallel, Ms. Melody provided an update to the broader Payroll audience via a staff meeting. In the meeting, she confirmed the agreement of the proposed change. Ms. Melody felt confident that the only audience impacted by the changes being pursued was production and that it made life easier for them but felt a confirmation needed to occur. During that presentation, Ms. Melody was reminded through feedback that the Maintenance team should be consulted since they are also impacted by weekend coverage needs, a key element of what has been going wrong. Ms. Melody will be bringing in a representative from Maintenance to discuss plans and determine if they should be a part of the core or extended team as well as a final solution approval stakeholder.

Note that in this example, having a conversation with another department (working cross-functionally) relaying concerns of wasted time is a critical conversation that needed to take place. Communication was a key factor here and it took both parties to seek the win-win. Having discussions about wasted time can backfire but when done constructively, it is the first step to finding solutions for holistic improvement. We must exploit these opportunities to drive improvements and help our teams work more efficiently and effectively. We can never know where the next best idea will come from. Egos get in the way of free-thinking and progress so let's put the pride aside.

__Coach's Note:__ Perhaps you've heard the story where it was discovered (a little too late) that New York City's Lincoln Tunnel clearance was too low for a certain tractor-trailer load and it got stuck. It was a little girl caught in the backed-up traffic that suggested letting the air out of the tires then backing the truck out. We couldn't confirm the validity of this story but it makes a great point so we'll run with it. Good ideas can come from anywhere and at any time.

Step 4 – Defining our Project Charter

Now that we have decided on our lead project, it's time to roll up our sleeves. In this step, we build out our objective, business case, team and certain logistics. Before we do anything, it's important to consider why we'd want to take on an initiative? From a business perspective, what are the compelling reasons to work on a certain project?

At this juncture, there should be at least two compelling reasons for this project; one, because it aligns with our overarching strategic priorities and two because it is causing us the most (or nearly the most) pain. These items create our business case. Continuing through this phase of the project, the "Define Phase," we want to; decide on our problem statement, determine who is the right team to work on the problem, and determine the objective for the effort. We'll pull the team together for a kick-off meeting, and confirm these aspects, gain commitment and establish our logistics as well as the team's deliverables.

In the kick off meeting we decided to pull together a representative from IT, Manufacturing and Purchasing. We need to share the concept we are considering and some hunches about what we might find. The goal of the meeting is to align through the solidification of our Charter Document. We'll determine our deliverables and script our next steps.

By the way, the Maintenance team determined that if Manufacturing was happy, it would satisfy their needs as well and won't actively participate in the team.

Sample Charter Document Template

Topic	Notes to prompt adaptation to your project.
Project Name	Payroll and Time Card Project
Customer	Who is the recipient of the output of this effort?
Sponsor	Who is the primary leader providing the resources for this effort? Should a disagreement arise, the sponsor could be leveraged for escalation.
Project Champion	Who is the facilitator guiding the activities for this effort?

Business Case	Describe why this is a good opportunity for the company. Quantify the opportunity and the expected gains (ROI).
Problem Statement	Whether the effort has been put in place to resolve a suddenly arising problem or an improvement opportunity, specifically state the problem this team is intending to resolve. Name the process, quantify the opportunity and reference dates as accurately as possible. Revisit the problem statement to ensure continued alignment through the project.
Deliverables	How will the team determine the successful completion of the effort? What needs to be completed? Be specific and quantify what success looks like. This piece becomes powerful when the team is ready for sunset. Ambiguity here can create misalignment with sponsors and customers, a common pitfall. Remember, err on the side of under-promising (without sandbagging) and over-delivering.
Feedback Plan	How will you receive and incorporate input from the appropriate stakeholders at the onset of the project as well as with solution iterations on the way to formal completion and deployment?
Scope	**In Scope** - List what is within the scope of this team. Leverage your process flow chart. Be clear where the process begins and ends for this effort. Refer to this regularly to ensure the team is on track. **Not In Scope** - List what is not in the scope of this team. Ideas will come up that will tend to increase the scope. Consider a bin list for follow up

	enhancements that get captured clearly in the project closure phase.
Team Members	**Core Team Members:** Individually list your project's core team members. **Extended Team Members:** Individually list as appropriate. **Stakeholders:** Who should be considered important relative to this change? Do you need a plan to address them and their concerns?
Meeting Logistics	**Logistics** • Weekly on Tuesdays at 2:00 pm for 1 hour • Room will be scheduled in your digital calendar

	Standing Agenda
	• Action Item Review
	• Hot Topics, News, Updates and Announcements
	• Project Review
	    o Status
	    o Accomplishments since last meeting
	    o Plans and expectations between now and next meeting
	    o Barriers
	    o Help needed
	Note: The above is the standing agenda, individual meeting details will be updated in the calendar with ample warning for preparation.

Effective Meetings	**Effective Meeting Principles will be used** • Facilitator • Scribe - Takes minutes, action items, etc. • Time Keeper - Keeps to agenda schedule

	• Gatekeeper - Keeps group on the topic **Note**: If you cannot attend a meeting please notify the facilitator to see if accommodations can be made. Substitute representation is not appropriate for this effort.

We have at least a brief business case quantifying what we expect to gain through this effort. We've aligned the team through a problem and resulting goal statement. We've established expectations for each role on the team as well as the logistics for how the team will work together. We've define the deliverables for the effort and have an estimate of how long the effort will take.

Now is a good time to leverage some of the tools that we've learned. Let's map our process flow in the kick-off meeting so that the whole team is on the same page. This will also assist us in filling out our charter document.

Process Flow Diagram – **Payroll**

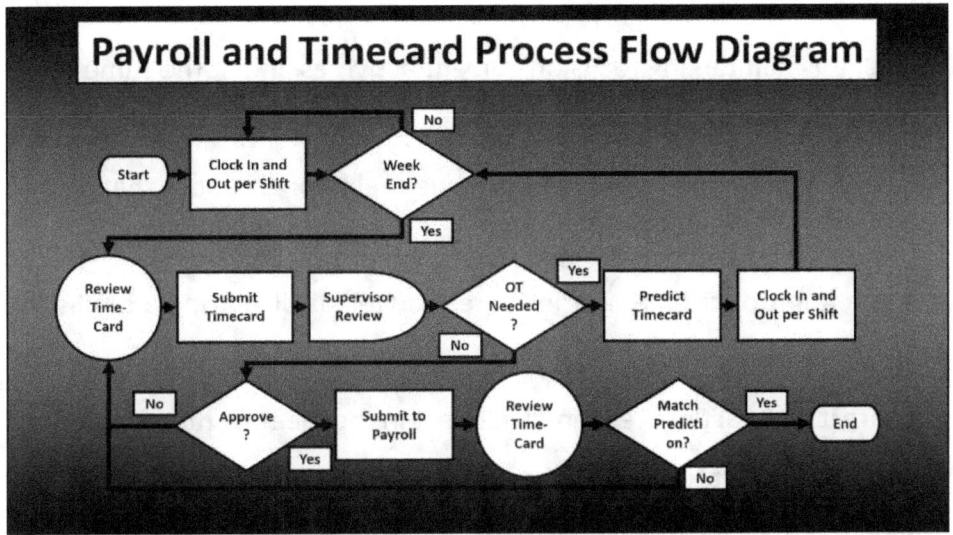

Okay, putting our process into a flow diagram has created the proper mindset to perform our waste walk. Recall Dot.Wimpie (affectionately referred to as Dottie) and review the process as accurately as possible. Do you see any waste? Would your customers, colleagues, or peers? Do you have any recent complaints or other collected information you can review? Make a note of each item.

In this case, big opportunities present themselves through inspections and a large opportunity comes at the activity of predicting the overtime and then having it match the submission. It strikes us a system originally conceived in distrust. It seems that significant opportunities exist in that area.

Remember, this is an iterative process and keeping notes will be critical for maintaining focus on current activities and at the same time, not losing sight of good ideas. As we walk through our process flow, it might remind us of a myriad of items we feel strongly about that do not relate to the particular phase or tool we are currently working with. Make a habit of capturing brief notes as well as displaying a bin list of ideas. When someone states they'll take care of doing something, capture it as an action item and include it in the meeting minutes. When a good idea is stated, allow the discussion to continue as you get up, traverse the area to the whiteboard and add the idea to a growing list of ideas for pursuit. At a future time, the team can discuss any project management details related to it.

Check Point

Before we move on to the next step, it's important to consider if the right things have been put in place to ensure success. Have we built a compelling business case that supports putting energy into this initiative? Do we have the right team members and are they all on board? Do they understand their role and commitment? Are the deliverables well-articulated and documented to ensure agreement at project closure? If these things are in place, that's great, let's move forward. Again, the process is iterative and moving backward to clarify is as appropriate as you believe it needs to be.

Coach's Note: Keep in mind that we want to complete our project. Going backward is ok and should be considered relative to ROI. One properly completed project is far greater than any amount of started projects that never make it across the finish line.

Chapter 4 – Measure and Quantify

Since we are only interested in the truth, we must pursue a data-driven approach. Therefore, the next thing we need to do is establish a baseline set of indicators and then drive improvement in them. If you are not familiar with the term baseline in this context, it means creating a standard set of measurements and then monitoring the process for a period of time to observe how the process normally behaves. There is a statistical concept that states all processes have noise. Monitoring our process will help us understand the noise in our process. After we make good change, we'll continue to collect the measurements to confirm that any changes we make have a positive impact relative to our baseline set of indicators.

In an effort to understand the current performance of our process, we'll need to make some decisions about how best to measure our process. For example, we wouldn't use a tape measure to measure the width of an atom and we wouldn't use a microscope to measure the length of our car. In our case, we simply used time in hours (or portions of hours) and logged each individual occurrence.

Why Quantify?

Let's be honest, if we ask five people what we should work on first, we'll get five different answers, maybe six. If we ask five people how much time a step in our process takes, we'll get five different answers for that too. What is the probability that they are all correct? The answer is zero and that is why we need to quantify. We cannot base our career, our P&L, and the future on gut feel or innuendo.

Perhaps a system already exists that can provide us with the unbiased perspective (raw data) needed to affect real change. If no system exists then consider creating a simple manual tracking sheet to categorize and quantify your processes of consideration like we did to get us this far. Manual tracking sheets are commonly used as a data collection system that can help flush out the right place to begin. Like all measurement systems, yours may need a revision or two before it works as well as we might like. No worries though, good information can be garnered rapidly and point us in a solid direction. Avoid waiting for the perfect system or other forms of action blocking procrastination or paralysis. Begin when your system is considered about 80% accurate. Even if our data isn't perfect, our current measurement capability ought to be good enough to detect a shift in the right direction and that's a good beginning.

If you already have a data collection system, take the time now to ensure it works well for you. Remember, the data you collect moving forward should stand the test of time. Continuously modifying your data collection system disrupts the ability to look at long term trends which is a form of data manipulation. A strong goal to have in the back of your mind would be to demonstrate improvement in process with long term trends born out of real effort invested in good change. These types of impacts are the types that promotions and merit increases need to have some basis in. If your company has been around for years, then most, if not all, critical processes should be trend-able by years.

We'll make the assumption that a spreadsheet program is available and that the reader is versed in using it. The data collection sheet we created earlier will be leveraged to learn about associated opportunities for improvement.

Check Point

Before we move to the next step (Analysis), let's consider a few things. Have we determined what we want to learn about relative to our process? Have we accurately captured the truth? Have we developed clear, unambiguous operational definitions for the categories or attributes we wish to measure? Have we made a reasonable choice between leveraging existing data versus gathering new data? Have we run a pilot confirming that our data collection system is doing what we expect? In other words, are we getting consistent measurement results from all people involved in measuring?

If these items are satisfied, then it makes sense to move on to the next phase.

Chapter 5 – Analyze - Improve Your Understanding

Before we go much further let's make sure we understand the need for an unbiased data collection system.

E.E. Cummings said, "Always the beautiful answer who asks a more beautiful question." We began with this end in mind back when we designed our data collection template. We gathered data such that we could expose the opportunities hidden within it. As we move through the analysis phase, it will become apparent that certain opportunities for collecting all the right data may have been missed.

Coach's Note: *Be careful, it is very easy to fall into the loop and trap of wanting more data, analyzing it and wanting more data. Said no engineer ever, "I just need a little more time to understand the data." Keep your eye on the goal. In fact, now is a good time to review your problem statement and weigh it against the critical concept of 'time to market.' We must be reminded to ask ourselves, do we have the data necessary to impact good change relative to our problem statement? There's no issue with expanding the scope if that makes sense. Just honor the decision and consider the ROI and schedule impact.*

Let's keep things clean and simple as we bear in mind the old adage, 'garbage in, garbage out.' The phrase simply means that the accuracy of the decisions we make coming out of our analyzed data is directly proportional to the accuracy of the data going in. If we took a low energy approach and asked people how long it takes to do something, then we are really asking for their opinion. From experience, those responses provided are rarely within 10% of actual (try it sometime). Leaving it up to a conversational estimate or gut feel can often have you working from the wrong perspective and on the wrong things. So too can reacting to people's well-meaning but relatively arbitrary input. Again, our goal is to affect real change and by necessity, real change comes from real intelligence researched from unbiased systems. Grab a stopwatch (your phone) and measure like the famed caped crusader, --with science!

When you can share the projects you are or will be, working on and how they are prioritized based on data, people will stop telling you what you should be doing and you become the captain of your own ship. Try this a few times and watch your circle of influence grows. Share your list and demonstrate that you are acceptable to input and accountable for your output. Grow your career based on tangible and meaningful accomplishments.

We'll take the existing set of data and filter it so that we can review just the Payroll portion. We graph it because a picture is worth a thousand words and the resulting picture looks like the following. Note that when we are sharing our information, our tables of data should be easily accessible if supporting details are required for discussion. Having summarized data available in back up slides can be helpful and build credibility with your audience.

Payroll Interruption Trend and Pareto

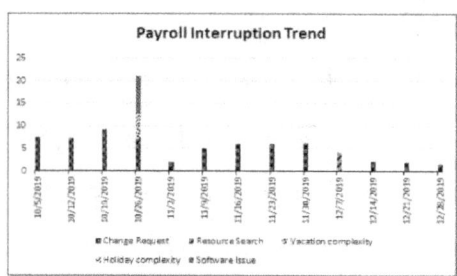 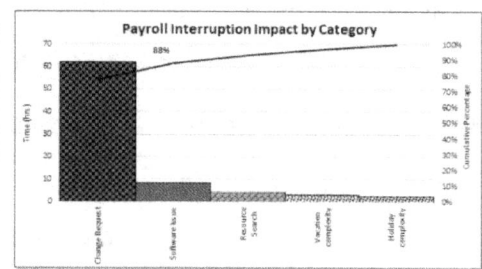

Okay, now that we have established our baselining look at our data, the next thing we need to do is analyze it. We should think about indicators from two different perspectives. First, there is the data, graphs, and charts appropriate to management reviews. Then there are data, graphs, and charts relative to the process owner and their intent to listen to their process and drive improvements. We should look to eliminate waste and only collect the information we need but the process owner should always be trying to anticipate the next level of answers needed relative to their process.

Consider that all indicators need to be studied on their own merits. If we are new to monitoring our process then we'll take what we can get and bias for action.

Lean Thinking in Human Resources: A Great Place to Begin

Coach's Note: *If nice was an option, it would be nice to have fifty-six weeks of data. The reason for thirteen months is because that often represents a time frame needed to clearly demonstrate improvement as well as show where you were at this time last year. Weekly summations are key because in most data, tracking by days can be too noisy and trending by month doesn't tell you what you need to know fast enough or with enough granularity. Regardless, if you do a good job of capturing the data at the individual level, it can easily be configured to show it in a way that makes the most sense for your situation.*

Step 5 – Learning from our Factual Information

If the word, 'analyze' strikes fear into you, don't be alarmed. If you are not a big fan of math, that's okay. We won't get deep. Further, if you are good at math and spreadsheets, it will be apparent where and how to apply them.

Coach's Note: *There is usually someone in finance or engineering who can assist you with creating the below in a spreadsheet and show you how to update it with continued data collected. It would take someone familiar with spreadsheets about thirty minutes (at the most) to set this data collection template up and share how to update it. For personal growth, you might consider asking about or researching pivot tables, a very powerful tool for analysis. Once the spreadsheet is set up with the* *proper data collection approach (as shown), updating or adjusting is easy.*

By reviewing the data in this form and reviewing the notes associated with each line of data entered, ideas for improvement will arise. Capture those ideas in a bin list for consideration in the next phase.

The FourUp - Review of Our Process

Let's walk through a four-part system we'll call the FourUp. Each piece of the four-part system works together and provides a great overview of the process as well as the work being done to improve the process.

Quadrant I - Histogram

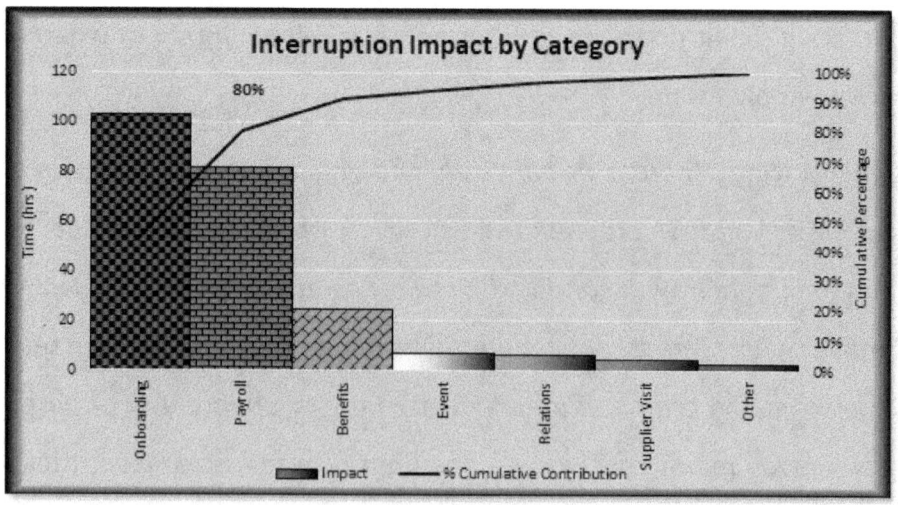

Quadrant I – Quadrant I of the FourUp demonstrates a histogram (or Pareto) of the frequency of issue occurrence by category. We sorted the information from highest to lowest frequency for ease of priority understanding. A Pareto analysis of the data demonstrates where the most "pain" is being experienced. In this case, pain is quantified in total time (hours) on the left axis. This could easily be converted to dollars and use a burden rate for each role captured in the data but let's keep it in hours here.

Note that the axis on the right side of this graph demonstrates the accumulated percent of impact. Commonly referred to as the eighty-twenty (80/20) rule, the reader can witness the application of the discovery that the Italian finance expert, Vilfredo Pareto , made. Here, approximately 80 percent of our pain is being caused by 20 percent of the categories. It turns out that in general, quantification by category follows the eighty-twenty rule. This is an important concept because knowing this ensures focus and that we work on the right things in the right order.

To share more on relative language (engineering slang if there is such a thing), that drop in the Pareto from Payroll to Benefits is referred to as the difference between cliff and rubble. This is the separating point between the critical few and the trivial many. For example, taking on an effort to improve the supplier visit process would be wasteful because relative to Onboarding and Payroll, it just not worth the effort right now. We will gain far more by staying focused on Onboarding and Payroll. Often, folks get caught up in working on the trivial many because they don't have a process in place to help them understand where the most pain is coming from.

Quadrant II - Trend

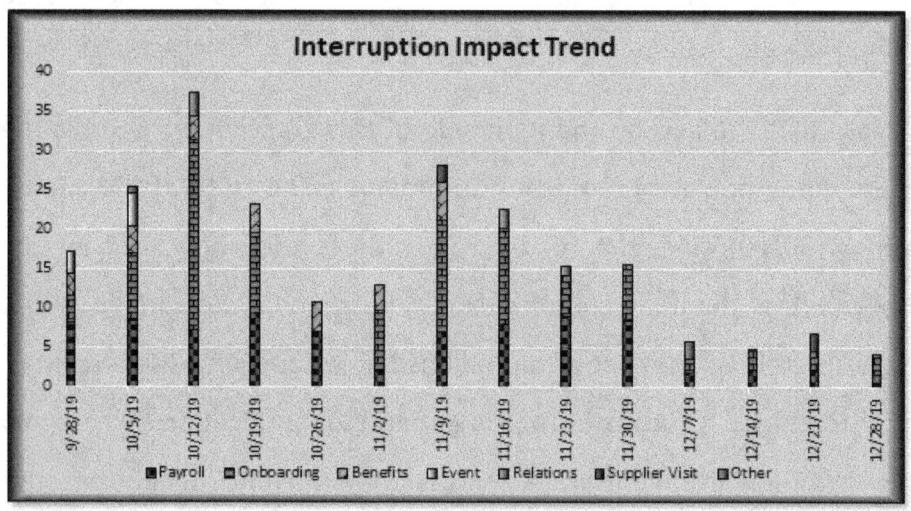

Quadrant II – Here the data depicts how each category of pain has been experienced over time. Each column of data represents a week's worth of collected information. We've leveraged a stacked bar chart to illustrate the categories individually within each week's bar. From this view, we gain the perspective of timing.

Lean Thinking in Human Resources: A Great Place to Begin

Quadrant III – Project List

ID	Impact Category	Action Description	ECD	Completed
A	Onboarding	Modify new employee training to include reference.	11/15/2019	11/7/2019
B	Onboarding	Work with IT to configure new computers with printer.	12/7/2019	Open
C	Payroll	Modify time card submission cut-off time.	11/15/2019	12/1/2019
D	Benefits	Improve logic for web page per customer feedback.	1/7/2020	Open
E	Benefits	Create a Frequently Asked Quuestions page.	1/7/2020	Open

Quadrant III – This table represents current and anticipated projects, their Estimated Completion Dates (ECD) as well as their targeted category of impact. Used well it will demonstrate your plan and priorities. Sharing this information openly tends toward having the effect of being left alone by your peers because you have demonstrated your focus, the reasons for it, and current actions. Peers will move toward patience and allow you and your team, the time needed to execute the projects. You will be seen as a leader based on sound decision making. Isn't that what we all want to see from our leaders? Remember, micromanagement is most often born out of issues of trust. This approach garners trust and inspires others to similar thinking.

Quadrant IV – Source Data and Implementation

Categories	9/28/2019	10/5/2019	10/12/2019	10/19/2019	10/26/2019	11/2/2019	11/9/2019	11/16/2019	11/23/2019	11/30/2019	12/7/2019	12/14/2019	12/21/2019	12/28/2019	Grand Total
Benefits	2.7	3.4	3.1	3.5	3.7	3.2	4.8								24.4
Event	2.9	4.1													7.0
Onboarding	4.0	6.1	14.2	8.6		7.8	11.1	7.3	5.2	7.2	1.9	2.6	2.6	2.6	81.1
Payroll	10.1	9.6	9.2	11.0	8.0	7.0	10.0	7.9	9.0	8.4	1.7	2.2	2.0	1.5	97.6
Relations			2.9					2.3	1.1						6.3
Termination		0.8									2.8				3.6
Supplier Visit							2.2						2.2		4.4
Grand Total	19.7	24.0	29.4	23.1	11.7	18.0	25.9	19.7	15.3	15.6	6.4	4.8	4.6	6.3	224.4

Quadrant IV – This table demonstrates the actual data used to make up Quadrant I and II. Further, it shows the week a project was completed by correlating a subscript identifier, in this case, a dot, that correlates with the implementation of the related project. The impact the project made can be seen by looking at the difference in the data after the project was implemented.

The FourUp Summarized – Following represents a singular view that tells a powerful and comprehensive story.

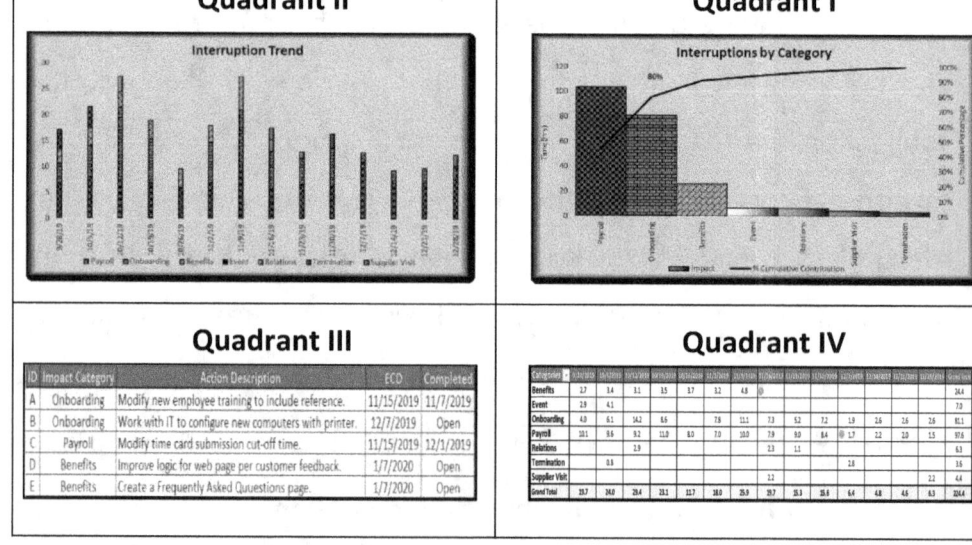

The Benefits of the FourUp

The FourUp is a very powerful way to demonstrate your process and associated efforts. It employs a holistic perspective of your process and work being invested in improving those processes. It gives you the opportunity to demonstrate your competency for your process and your motivation to improve through fact-based prioritization.

Individually, each of the charts are good but used together they tell a much larger and more powerful story. The FourUp charts and tables work together and the power of what is displayed here has been a critical business tool to world-class companies for many years.

There's a saying that "data have no meaning apart from its context." If we look at Quadrant I without Quadrant II, we are robbing ourselves of the perspective of timing. If we look at Quadrant II without looking at Quadrant I, we are robbing ourselves of the perspective of quantity. For example, if you review Quadrant I (the Pareto) by itself you will be led to believe that Benefits are the number three impact on time however when you review it with Quadrant II, you will notice that it hasn't been a problem since 11/9/2019. You may then recall that the company switched benefit providers and their website is far more customer-centric quickly answering frequently asked questions the HR had to respond to in the past. Discussions with employees could confirm the improvement. Imagine if the frequency of issues was larger, without knowing the timing associated with it, an organization could take on an effort to resolve something that is no longer an issue.

The FourUp should be considered a standard approach to introducing indicators and the resulting actions associated with the insight they provide. This data should then be followed by the details of the projects being resourced to positively impact the indicators. The FourUp would be presented in one slide and then follow up slides would provide clarity on each active project, accomplishments made to date, challenges encountered or barriers to progress, next steps, and help needed. This approach follows the *"be brief, be bright, and be gone"* model for updating groups/leadership. The majority of any discussion should revolve around the help needed portion of the presentation.

__Coach's Note:__ The FourUp is the antidote to micromanagement. If you think about it, micromanagement is often a response by the supervisor for lack of trust in an employee. By demonstrating your focus and progress you've created trust and integrity. If that doesn't get the boss of your back, resort to physical violence. Legal disclaimer #121217 - We're joking!

Presenting the FourUp

Consider the data-based logic in the following explanation to a group of senior managers viewing this FourUp.

"As you will observe in the Pareto view of the data, the number one and two sources of interruptions for the Human Resource group is On-Boarding and Payroll.

We recognized that a quick win was available by prioritizing effort for Payroll even though it was number two on the Pareto . A solution could be quickly implemented here as opposed to an On-Boarding effort where significant investment is needed to update corollary training and support documentation. We launched Project C with the intent of being completed on 11/15/2019 however the needed adjustments in the server were pushed for competing priorities in IT. Regardless, the associated training material, work instructions and general marketing of the change took place and the system went live during the week of 11/1/2019. Quadrant IV demonstrates an immediate drop in time requirements from an average of 7.4 hours per week to 1.9. That's about a 75% reduction in effort freeing up time needed to pursue our organization-wide Lean initiative.

We'd like to thank you all for your support of this change, especially our production managers who spent the most time working with payroll to get time accurate for their teams. We hope you'll agree this effort is a win across the organization.

Our next project will address onboarding. We've already started on the charter document. Ms. Melody will be championing the effort. The next slides layout the plan and the anticipated help we are requesting.

By the way, notice that Benefits related issues hasn't been a problem since the FAQs webpage was implemented the week of 11/9/2019 demonstrating a solid solution for all of us."

Check Point

Before we move past the analysis phase, we'll want to make sure of a few things. Have we thoroughly reviewed our process? Our measurement system is giving us accurate information. We understand our process at a deeper level because of good questions born out of quantified research. We've identified waste form multiple perspectives and most especially our customers. We've narrowed our scope to the critical few root causes.

Chapter 6 - Improve

Three Ways to Improve your Indicators

Previously we discussed how good data gets us to the heart of the matter and helps identify what can be affected to impact your indicators in the right direction. The next thing we want to do is take action to drive those indicators. There are three ways to improve organizational indicators. You can manipulate your data, you can manipulate your process, or you can make good change.

One - Manipulate your Data.

Changing aspects of the data to improve its appearance or hide negative events such as filtering out time frames or an underperforming employee are examples of manipulated data. It distorts the truth and will lead to misinformed decision making for the business.

Two - Manipulate your Process.

Altering a process to artificially create the desired outcome is a form of process manipulation. For example, changing the order of questions in a survey used that has been used for the past five years to have a reminder of a holiday party right in front of the question that asks if management cares about creating a fun work environment could lead survey-takers to enter a higher score. Reporting it out as an improvement in workforce relations though nothing relevant has changed is considered manipulating the process. Saving easy jobs for the end of the month to bulk release in order to achieve heroic output and superhero status relative to monthly goals is also an example of manipulating the process.

Three - Make Good Change.

Making good change means leveraging the truth, understanding process deficits and working to make improvements that positively affect output.

Please note that two of the above improvement methodologies are easy and unfortunately, all too commonly implemented. Taking shortcuts eventually catches up with us and a disciplined approach always wins out over the long term, -ask the tortoise. Whether in the corporate world or in the fitness center, we get the results we deserve.

It's still true, there are no silver bullet solutions (or perhaps the silver bullet is problem-solving) and making good change takes well-placed effort and relentless pursuit of better and better. Think of it this way, if we're not working on the right thing, we're working on something. Even if that is trying to look busy, it takes effort. We might as well work on a priority that helps us all. The job we save may be our own.

Keep in mind that good problem-solving is born out of data and avoids the trap of gut feel, squeaky wheel, pet projects, and innuendo. Important at this phase is to review the "Bin List" of ideas you've been collecting as you progressed through each of the prior steps. Review the indicators and what they're trying to tell you, review feedback from customers and suppliers to the process. Are there any complaints that have been formally captured? Last but not least, brainstorm with a diverse set of perspectives, what could be done to make appropriate impacts.

Okay, now it's time to do our waste walk. Recall Dot.Wimpie (affectionately referred to as Dottie) and physically review the process. Do you see any waste? Would your customers, colleagues, or peers? Do you have any recent complaints or other collected information you can review? Make a note of each item that should be considered for improvement in your bin list.

Step 6 – Problem-Solving

The information portrayed in the FourUp previously presented was created to simulate projects and illicit understanding. Taking a closer look at the data collection tables and notice that a sub-category has been captured to assist direction. We have the data and we've analyzed it. From it we have determined and prioritized the sources of our pain.

We've leveraged our decision matrix to help us decide where to place our energy first. The decision matrix identified a quick hit opportunity in regards to Payroll. This is the step we've been planning to get to. Now that we have the decision matrix filled out, we also have a strong set of projects planned for the future as resources become available.

Recall the Bin List of improvement ideas we've been collecting? Now is the time to leverage it because this is when we'll gather all ideas and categorize them or group them with like solutions. We'll also want to take our fresh perspective, past issues, and brainstorm solutions.

Tool – Brainstorming

Remember, the beginning portion of brainstorming is free and creative thinking. The team should be guided to build on ideas, not shoot them down (the gunslinger approach). There will be plenty of time later to filter but it may be the crazy ideas that initiate the one that leads to breakthrough performance. Keep brainstorming fast, upbeat and moving forward. Once an exhaustive list of ideas is complete, each team member can cast three (to five) votes for the projects they feel will have the best impact on the problem needing to be resolved. Usually, a solution will present itself however this can be a good time to leverage the decision-making matrix. It's at about this time that the crazy ideas will naturally filter themselves out.

Table: Sample Brainstorm List of Ideas and Votes Acquired

Idea	Votes
Modify cutoff time for final timecard entry	5
Have manager do all time cards	1
Put everyone on salary	0
Modify start and end week day	2
Other…	NA

Action here or action there? That is the question.

Nothing is harder than avoiding real work. Consider that the typical day of an HR professional is split into at least three categories; the projects that get your group closer to your long term vision, the sustaining activities required by the role and the unplanned interruptions. If we avoid good change and all other things remain the same, then simple math says unplanned interruptions cannot decrease in frequency. When focus is derailed from the activities already on your plate there's the impact of time of the interruption plus the time of the response and also the momentum of thought. Sometimes getting back into the flow of the activity is not easily recovered, then when effort gains flow again, bang, another interruption. Spend too much time in this cycle and the average person begins their downward spiral of feeling like they never get anything done. Eventually, they feel overwhelmed. This cycle is very taxing on personal morale which leads to a negative impact on all who interact with you. We all want to be a part of a winning team. Winning teams tend to attract and retain good people.

Coach's Note: *Too many companies either do not understand that good change is the right path to long term prosperity or are convinced it's too hard. Yes, it takes a bit of effort but don't convince yourself that you can't before you realize that you can. Truly, once you make good change a habit, it's simple and repeatable. Especially in the early stages where there can be orchards full of low hanging fruit. This is the approach of working smarter, not harder.*

Whatever we choose to implement, we want to consider documented support structures. They have to update with the change. We should update related training material and roll out the training if appropriate. Are there work instructions, procedures, and policies? Ensure questions are asked and answered prior to the cutoff time. Give your customers or at least a representative subset of your customers an opportunity to review the changes prior to going live with them.

Check Point

There are some gates that should be satisfied in the improve phase before moving to the next phase. Did we brainstorm a list of ideas and then screen them to ensure the best idea(s) is pursued. Did we develop a plan for piloting and testing the solution(s) prior to implementing them? Did we create the future state process flow diagram that will help us gain insight into all items needing to be addressed for proper implementation? Did we perform some type of review with key stakeholders to ensure all risks are known and appropriately addressed? Did we ensure the solution addresses the original problem statement and agreed-upon deliverables?

Chapter 7 - Control

Step 7 – Chock the Wheels of Progress

Now that you've put energy in place and deployed the new system, it's critical to make sure that what you've created doesn't unravel and slide back to the original process. The most difficult phase of making any change can be sustaining it. This phase is where we chock the wheels of progress. We put systems in place to ensure the gains we made stay in place, scale with our growth and continuously improve. To sustain the change, it is important to weave our solutions into the fabric of the process(es) and systems that exist. If there are related work instructions, procedures, policies, websites and/or public files in place they must be a part of the implementation plan. Support structures like process reviews, business reviews, business update meetings, etc. must incorporate the new expectations.

Update training, work instructions, etc. to lock in the learning through the systems that support it. Consider other support systems that might need engagement/updating like IT or suppliers. Your effort will be proving that this isn't the flavor of the month, that it's real and that you intend to lock it in and keep forward progress via the next project on the list. Start soliciting input to demonstrate your desire for active engagement. That people can impact good change from everywhere in the company.

Coach's Note: *If a change is not well deployed, it might as well not have been done in the first place. How often do we hear employees being blamed for not knowing certain information? The control phase is the part where we, as leaders of change, take ownership and set them up for success. They are our customers and are expected to be experts in their processes, not ours. It's up to us to make our systems easy to understand and easy to be successful in.*

A word on deployment. Getting the word out on the new system requires a bit of an advertising campaign. So get your elevator speech together and have something good to say, say it well, and say it often.

Aside from various forms of support structures already mentioned, monitoring our indicators after the implementation is a method of process control. Properly set up and regularly reviewed, monitoring will confirm our change didn't create an unexpected negative impact or create a new issue. That indeed, we've made a good change.

There is always stress to go back to the way things were. Be reminded that it takes twenty-one days to change behavior (even our own). So take the time to build the system such that it will last the test of time. Review the change regularly during those first twenty-one days (at least) and demonstrate continued support through speaking with your process customers and share indicators. Follow up with the changes that may have been on the bin list and were not able to be pursued during the change event. Maintain contact with your customers and continue to drive the well-crafted message.

Further, continue to consider your change and what could go wrong. Where are the risks? Anticipate potential failures and then ask yourself how bad it could be and what would need to be put in place to avoid it or otherwise react quickly and appropriately.

Critical Concept - Regular Reports

Reporting out regularly to various audiences is another form of a control system. It keeps the process owner's finger on the pulse of the system. It reminds folks to bring up issues that may have been observed and allows us to promptly resolve them before they get out of control. Good information provided by a system based in unbiased truth leads to good questions and good questions lead to good change driving the organization toward good growth and improved competitiveness. In the end, everyone wins; the employee, the department, the organization, the community, the nation. If that seems a little "motherhood and apple pie," then take a look at the evolution of many leading countries. How did culture affect the fastest growing countries?

FourUp

Recall the FourUp previously discussed. This information, at the right level, is a critical part of the control phase. It demonstrates that you are regularly reviewing the status of your processes and have a continuous flow of projects that target improvement in a prioritized manner. Sharing the right level of information regularly will solidify your competency, garner respect and influence your position in the organization.

Critical Concept - Seek Feedback

Critical to making good change is keeping communication channels open with your customers. You'll want to understand the impact of the changes you make. Keep in mind however that one piece of bad feedback should not unravel the work you've done. Statistically speaking, one or a few bits of negative feedback is just that, a few data points. Human nature tends to be silent when things go well and negative when it's not exactly as desired. Pulse your customers and ask them if they've had a chance to use the new system. Results could solidify the change or lead to an iteration furthering the improvement. Regardless, have pride and own your process with the intent to continuously improve it. That's the behavior good leaders are made of.

At the same time, continuous improvement is a journey and if your results made a significant impact on the pain being experienced, it may be appropriate to take those gains and move on to another item that is causing more pain. It is a cycle of taking the larger(est) Pareto item and eliminating or reducing it to be among the "rubble" of Pareto items. Then taking the next largest Pareto item and reducing/eliminating it. Then the next one and so on. It may sound cliché but it's a journey, not a destination. To add another cliché, it's a marathon, not a sprint. Keep moving forward and soon you will reap the benefits of all your focused hard work.

Coach's Note: *Imagine the waste of time if our new process reverts back to the old even though it is better. Consider how that could happen and what needs to be done to prevent it. Take a lesson from the Story of Cortez where he ordered his boats burned so that his men gave no thought of retreat. Perhaps that's a bit extreme but you get the idea. We all fear change to some degree. Put systems in place to keep the momentum moving forward.*

The control phase is where the legendary rubber hits the road. It is the system that ensures the powerful concept that outputs are as expected every time. Consider what good a change is if it never gets to your audience. It could be the best thing since sliced bread but if not well deployed, it should not have been done to begin with.

Regarding this change, there are a few things that should be done to ensure it is effective and well deployed. We should meet on the production floor to make sure everyone is comfortable with the change and knows how they interact. This should, of course, be done promptly, like at the end of the shift when and where the majority of users complete their timecard. Be present and engaged. Consider where else we should visit?

Critical Concept - MBWA

Management by walking around (MBWA) is a concept that reminds us to get out of our offices and go to where the work is happening. Here we'll use it as a method to engage with the customers of our output and their supervisors to ensure we have our finger on the pulse of the change. We'd like to hear that everything is going well and the intended audience is on board with the change, that they fully understand it and that we confirm we haven't unwittingly created a new issue implementing this one. Be warned, however, that we must be unbiased and listen for the facts, not for what we want to hear.

When all aspects of the Control Phase are completed you will be the beneficiary of a new system that gives you back time. In this case, almost a full day will be freed up through more accurate timecards at initial submission. Congratulations, you just improved your process's first pass yield.

Tool - Post Mortem

Whether you worked in a team or not, find the time to review the effort and the learning. We refer to this as the project post mortem, which may be a little dark, or the project critique. This will be a closed team discussion of what went well, what didn't go so well? What could be done better next time? What was learned? What should we do more of, less of? A list of pros and cons relative to the project along with a list of actions that can be implemented for future projects.

In this closed meeting, it will be important to establish an environment of trust so that people will share openly. There will invariably be things that didn't go as well as planned. Often, everyone knows it so get the details out, acknowledge it, solicit ideas for how to improve next time and don't belabor the negative. Confrontations happen in team environments and organizational development models acknowledge that no team can get to the performing phase if the team doesn't go through storming phase. This is a great way to acknowledge the past and move on from it. Reiterate the beneficial learnings that came from those honest and often passionate discussions.

Celebrate with the team. Remind them of the trials, the tribulations. How did the team progress? What were critical moments that helped the team progress? Where there any, "Aha!" moments? How did you get to them? Was it easy or did it come from some hard work or edgy discussions? Did things always go perfectly? How did that affect the team's development in the short term, the long term? What new things did we learn about our process? Did we incorporate appropriately so they are retained? What things did we learn about problem-solving, project management?

This is also a great time to reward team members for their contributions. This doesn't have to mean cash or plaques. We know of one gangly engineering manager that used to give popular metal die cast cars for lack of any budget as a symbol of appreciation. He claimed his teams were, *"Race Ready!"* and team members would collect and display their trophy cars proudly. It's the genuine appreciation that means the most.

This is also the time to officially closeout the team's charter document as successfully meeting the objective and formally disband. Follow up with closing minutes capturing the post mortem and stating the completed deliverables as the final formal detail.

Chapter 8 – Benefits

The Benefits of Lean Learning

It matters less about where you start and more that action is taken. The process is self-improving and self-fulfilling. As you approach and resolve the first issue of focus, your effort will drive establishing a better queue of the next objectives. Even if you are off the mark on a first or any project, taking action leads you to learn and learning drives better direction and goal setting. Lack of action, lack of decision making can single-handedly kill a company.

__Coach's Note:__ Kathy Reichs said, "Indecision is the key to flexibility." It's funny but all too often decisions don't get made and put companies at risk of missing key opportunities.

As you've journeyed your way through this book, you have immersed yourself in problem-solving techniques leveraged frequently in the technical world. We have intended to present this in a non-technical and at least slightly entertaining manner while constructing improvement through a data-based approach.

Following this approach yields many benefits:

1) **Prioritized Action** - Protecting yourself and your team from the *"squeaky wheel"* syndrome. Having a prioritized list of projects

allows a data-based discussion to share where other's concerns are on the list. Even the CEO will understand that his/her recent concern may not be the highest priority and will be content to know that the concern is on the list and that it is queued for action. The CEO will also appreciate understanding that the concern is in the trivial many and that your focus is on the critical few. We would urge diplomacy here, however, the voice of reason is heavily laden with facts that would be hard to dispute.

2) **Performance Monitoring System** - Creation of a system that will enable you to continuously monitor the impact of the changes you make as well as the health of the process. Note that when the data is based in an automated collection system, it becomes simple to monitor the effectiveness of the change. If the data collection is manual, at some time after confirming the change is positive and sustainable, it may be appropriate to stop collecting that specific data. Continued energy here may not be well spent.

3) **Organizational Impact** - Working on the right things in the right order. Depending on objective this can free up your own time to stop spending so much energy in the urgent-unimportant so that you can make organizationally impactful changes at the next level. You're making your, and your team's, job easier, giving yourself the gift of time. Not only is this a proper impact on your annual review

and more important for the survival of the company but it's more rewarding to you as a professional. When you share your wins with new employees as well as across the entire organization, you are impacting the future of the company and culture. Incoming employees will understand that the expectation is woven into the fabric of the whole organization. This will very quickly have an impact on the future of the company.

4) **Expand your Influence** – The process improves self-awareness and gradually increases your impact on the organization. In time, there will be a recognition of improving competency and wisdom since you will be able to discuss processes at a deeper level of understanding. A customer-centric organization making good change inevitably achieves a state of recognition by those outside the unit. Your group will be sought out as much for the role you represent as well as the impact you enable and the ease of which it is to work with you. You've improved your ability to constructively and respectfully challenge all parts of the organization. You've demonstrated that yours is a professional position. You will be sought out by others to share what you know positioning you and your team for appropriate recognition.

Chapter 9 – Challenge

Now that you've made an impact within your world, consider the broader spectrum. Consider how you might build portions of what you've learned into annual reviews or the hiring system that defines the competencies your organization wants. Consider the hiring system that determines if certain desired behaviors are appropriately demonstrated like teamwork, an innate sense of the cost of quality, work ethic, continuous improvement, problem-solving ability, self-motivation, communication, integrity, working with ambiguity. Consider an onboarding system that trains employees to look for waste and enables them to be a part of the solution. Let new employees know how everyone contributes to creating a better version of the current company. Share success stories during onboarding to help drive the desired culture. Think of the possibilities.

Chapter 10 - Summary

Embrace that change is iterative and at some point, you may implement a change that didn't work out. It's okay, embrace the fact that standing in one place is worse than taking a wrong step. By taking action you've learned. By testing and measuring that action, you learned that better results can be found in a different direction. Celebrate noble failure.

Coach's Note: *How many ways does Thomas Edison know how not to make a lightbulb? Through a solid system of experimentation, test, measure and applied learning, you will be able to monitor impact and ensure that all communication channels are open for learning. You'll be engaged such that change that affects things negatively is recognized rapidly and corrective actions are swiftly implemented. Celebrate the learning and the journey. You know more because you took the first step, you're action-oriented, and adjustments can be made.*

If you only do continuous improvement events for yourself, you will be a more effective and efficient professional. If you influence your organization from your significantly interactive and therefore influential position, you'll be a game-changer for the good of the company as well as your own personal career. Be mindful that the real celebration is in the learning. A better understanding of the process improved, and the improvement process unleashes unlimited potential.

Leverage your new knowledge across the organization and learn to ask these five questions:
1. What problem are we trying to solve?
2. How will we improve or change the actual work?
3. How will we develop the people to be successful in the new system?
4. What leadership behaviors and management systems will be required?
5. What basic mindset or assumptions drive this transformation?

Also, remind folks to embrace discovery based on quantified information. Remind your team not to jump into solution space prematurely or be prescriptive without fully understanding the issue and the root cause. Role model how to begin with good questions and seek answers through data to drive and arrive at a better future state.

Customers will remember two things, really, really bad service and really, really good service. Otherwise, the days of patriotism to a brand are over. Make every experience with your customers a pleasure and they'll be back. Do the same for your suppliers as well. They often speak with or become your customers. The bottom line, good or bad performance will become your reputation in your industry. Be mindful of the shrinking world. Many are hungry for profitable opportunities.

The one thing. If you are going to remember one thing, remember that our employees are our greatest asset. Respect the individual. These are just tools. There is no substitute for collaboration with intelligent people motivated for a better future. A united approach to a shared destiny is a powerful thing. Good change starts with me and moves through us, together.

Chapter 11 - Problem-Solving Tools – Translation

While we were walking through this approach, the reader was learning well established and well regarded problem-solving tools commonly used in Structured Problem-solving, Lean, Six Sigma, 8D, CAPA, and other problem-solving methodologies. Many of the concepts may not be new to the reader. Often it's how they flow and work together that transforms the stand-alone tools into better business decisions and creates a more efficient organization.

Improved familiarity with the tools and concepts will also create a common language when working cross-functionally. More than taking interest, taking action such as that discussed in this book will improve mutual respect and bridge communication gaps that might exist in the organization. Many organizations use HR to implement policies and essentially, keep them out of trouble. However, the Human Resource professional can and should be a strategic weapon leveraged to win in business. If that is currently not the case, or could be improved, then strengthening cross-functional interactions through demonstrated improvement and accountability can be the first step toward achieving shared wins in a competitive world.

Leadership in our companies should consider the interaction the HR organization has with the team members their efforts are intending to reach. Archimedes said, "Give me a lever long enough and I shall move the world." Well, harnessing the HR professional is great leverage in the organization. Don't just be ready for your opportunities, find them.

DMAIC: DMAIC is an acronym used in Six Sigma (a problem-solving methodology) and it stands for Define, Measure, Analyze, Improve and Control. This book followed the methodology relatively closely. The supporting tools and concepts have been around for many years and again, we remain convicted to the flow being the key to success however any of the powerful tools can be leveraged at any time the situation calls for it. Think of them as if they are tools in a carpenter's tools belt. Use the tool that is needed at the time it is needed and allow it to scale with the situation. Too often we observed forced use of tools when the situation didn't call for it. Recall that people are our most valuable asset. Sound judgment based in a search for true understanding and a tenacious drive for improvement is the goal. The tools help us get there.

Value Stream Mapping: - Value Stream Mapping is a common phrase these days and simply refers to breaking down the process into steps. By laying out those steps in the order they are executed, a few things naturally occur. Inputs and outputs for each step are considered, boundaries become evident, a deeper understanding of each step gains focused discussion, suppliers, and customers of the process are considered. All of this leads to process understanding at a deeper level and often flushes out questions that lead to the next level of understanding. Deeper understanding fosters robust solutions.

Containment – The situational approach here had to do with taking on improvements and considering aspects of prevention rather than reacting to things that have gone wrong. A key difference between these two scenarios would be the need for containment when things go wrong. Theoretically, containment calls for accounting for what has gone wrong, what is going wrong and how to eliminate the continuation of it going wrong. It's a relatively straight forward concept but consider that we own a residential landscaping company and we just realized the fertilizer we use was contaminated and killing our client's grass. We'd need to know how many houses we service are in jeopardy for prompt corrective action, we'd need to stop all service calls requiring fertilizer until we have a solution, we'd have to quarantine all the fertilizer not used as well as share the information with the team to ensure they know what is going on and how to communicate with the customers. Containment occurs very early in the event (the Define phase). Otherwise, the approach to solving the problem at its root cause follows the same flow. As more information (Measure) is learned (Analyze) the proper response (Improve) can be deployed (Control).

The Learning Organization

A team that is always striving to be better thrives in learning and improves the caliber of their own workforce. When this is occurring, employees feel challenged and enjoy their work as well as their growing marketability. Good people deserve good opportunities and will aspire to new levels in the organization creating bigger impacts and further embed the culture. The best companies inspire their people to be the best version of themselves and harness their creative energy for a unified approach to a shared destiny.

Each tool presented offers more than just the merits of the tool itself. The discussions that occur during the use of these tools offer significant power that may not readily be understood. As you move through the process, especially with a team, discussions will reference back to places where tools were used making key points or challenging assumptions previously stated. Honor and enjoy the process. It is powerful on so many levels. Remember, we get the business we deserve.

End....

Epilogue

I've noticed over my career that the people that understand these tools and concepts the best often have the most humble responses when asked if they are familiar with continuous improvement and structured problem-solving methodologies. I've observed the most competent practitioners often respond with something along the lines of, *"I'm still learning."* It truly is a journey and I humbly submit that I too am still learning and ask that if you have any input relative to this book; positive or constructive, that you kindly send it to thejoysofbusiness@gmail.com with subject line "Lean Thinking in Human Resources." I look forward to hearing from you and would once again like to thank all that have shared their council over my career.

Thank you.

Acknowledgement

I would like to thank my mother and father for the positive impacts they have made on my life.

My mom (right-brained) for her wisdom, patience, and kindness. She had a way of asking the perfect question at the perfect time to help me uncover my own truths and discover who I was meant to be. Although no longer with us, she continues to be there every time I need her.

My father (left-brained) for his intelligence, perseverance and relentless tenacity to go after what you want in life. He is a role model for that, *"never give up, no quit"* attitude and he challenged me to do things I didn't know I could. He helped me discover that where there is a will, there is a way.

Both of my parents had a desire to make themselves better (lifelong learning) as well as a desire for adventure. Together they gave me the tools and confidence to embark on my adventures. I love you both dearly and truly appreciate the perspective I have because I've had each of you in my life.

Appendix A - Checklist for Problem-Solving

The Requirements of Good Change
1) Complexity is the enemy of action. Keep it simple, honor the process, and expand as you gain comfort and confidence.
2) Don't be too critical early in the process. It will stifle creative thinking that can lead to breakthrough achievements.
3) Honor what you know and do not know. Seek to improve understanding.
4) Define
    a. Strategy - Have a long term strategy and goals. Convert that into what it means for you and cascade to your team.
    b. Problem statement
    c. Objective
    d. Team
    e. Roles and Responsibilities
    f. Process Flow (process flow diagram)
5) Measure
    a. Data collection (reminder - trial your measurement system)
    b. Quantify the truth
        i. Data collection
        ii. Customer feedback
6) Analyze
    a. Entitlement comparison
    b. Benchmark comparison
    c. Histograms, trends and gap analysis
    d. Waste Walk
7) Improve
    a. Brainstorm
    b. Model
    c. 5S (is 5S right for you?)
    d. Iterative Solution Trials (test and measure)
        i. Pilot your change, seek feedback, modify as appropriate, re-deploy, and repeat as appropriate.
8) Control
    a. Monitoring
    b. Reports and reporting (FourUp Review)
    c. MBWA and campaigning the change
    d. Supporting document updates and deployment
    e. Training updates and deployment
    f. Acknowledging the team through presentation opportunities, accolades or other mentions
    g. Celebrate the learning

Appendix B – Offered Templates

Write to TheJoysOfBusiness@gmail.com with subject header "Lean Thinking in Human Resources" and then the specifics of why you are writing.

Consider a request for the following templates:

1. Charter Document Template

2. Toll Gate Checklist Template